Presented to

_____

on the occasion of

_____

by _____

Date _____

365
KIDS' CONFESSIONS
Making God's Word Personal in Little Lives

Written and compiled by

Virginia Goode Kite

Special thanks to *Julia Frolich*
for her contributions to the cover art.

ISBN 0-942847-02-4

* * * * *

Published by
Ron Kite Ministries & Publications
P.O. Box 33110
Tulsa, Oklahoma 74153

SECOND PRINTING MAY, 1992

TO: ***Deena,*** *the first who came to enrich our lives at age 10, expanding the walls of our "tent" and our heart;*

TO: ***John,*** *whose birth was a miracle gift from God, attained through prayer and confession, suffering and triumph, grace and mercy;*

TO: ***Glynndia,*** *who joined us next at age 6 and whose lively spirit provided the extra challenge I needed to keep me on my "spiritual toes."*

These are the inspiration for this book.
They taught me:
>   How to love beyond myself,
>   How to give more than I thought I was able,
>   How to believe God—for their lives, their health,
>   their peace, their development, their futures.

Thank you, Granddaddy Snyder,
For the love of God's Word which you instilled in me.
I hope Jesus can get a copy of this book to you.
                                        Love, Ginny

INTRODUCTION

Kids of today seem to have more ability, more potential, more God-given opportunities than ever before in man's history.

They also have more choices, more decisions, more temptations confronting them than any other generation.

It is absolutely imperative that parents teach their young ones from the cradle, so that they might be molded from earliest years into the image of Christ.

A vital part of that teaching must include daily exercise in learning, confessing, and utilizing God's Word.

Kids have an innate desire and urge to be aggressive. They are the upcoming soldiers of God's greatest army. Let us prepare them to use those aggressive potentials for God's glory, for victory in their lives, and that they may be a mighty force in this earth to overcome the last confrontation of the enemy.

Ginny Kite

FOREWORD: WHY CONFESSIONS?

Faith comes by *hearing and hearing* the Word of God. If a man believes in his heart and *confesses* with his mouth the Lord Jesus, he shall be saved. Whoever shall *speak* to the mountain shall have whatever he *says*. *

God intended for man to live by His Word. He gave us from earliest times a written record of His teachings—the Bible—and He has preserved it over the centuries. He clearly intended that we hear and learn and speak His living Word.

Man *is* what he believes, and he *becomes* what he confesses. When belief is weak, confession can make it stronger. Hearing the Word develops faith. Faith overcomes the weakness of the flesh.

Speaking the Word puts the devil on the run. When tempted by Satan in the wilderness, Jesus did what He now expects us to do: He used the Word of God coming through His own lips and verbally drove the devil off!

Teach your kids to pray daily. Teach them to read God's Word daily. And teach them how to use their spiritual authority by speaking God's Word daily over all situations. God's Word never fails!

> So shall My Word be that goes forth from My mouth; it shall not return to Me void, but it shall accomplish what I please, and it shall prosper in the thing for which I sent it.
> *Isaiah 55:11*

*Romans 10:17
Romans 10:9
Mark 11:23

How to Use KIDS' CONFESSIONS

A scripture confession is powerful. This book is loaded with God's POWER!

The 365 confessions in this collection can be used either by date reference, or by number reference. They are ordered by date for the convenience of those who like to have a dated devotional. But please don't limit the book by beginning only on January 1! It can be started any day of the year!

If you obtain the book in July, you can begin the child's daily confessions either with the date July 1, or with the numerical sequence beginning with Day "1."

The confessions are also listed in a Subject Index in back of the book. There will be many times you will want to recall a certain scripture, or have need of God's insight into a specific area. With the index, you will easily locate the scripture(s) you need.

The confessions can be used in the mornings to begin the day. They can be used to wind up early morning prayer or to precede or follow Bible storytime at night. They can even be used by the entire family as a short but dynamic group confession before the evening meal is shared together.

Appropriate scriptures and confessions can be used over and over. They can be taped to the mirror or recorded on the cassette player to minister to a specific area of need in a child. I have had successful experience in recording certain scripture confessions and replaying during the night on an auto-reverse tape player. The child's subconscious has been found to be a definite avenue by which he can receive positive reinforcement from God's Word.

This book is intended to be used by parent and child together. It should prove to be a fun activity which both child and parent will look forward to each day! The scripture reference can be read to the child, or a brief paraphrase given of the scripture, depending upon the child's age. Then, the confession should be read TO the child, phrase by phrase, so the child can easily repeat after you. *Use expression and emphasis so that the meaning can be grasped fully.* Concentrate on the child understanding and enjoying the confession. If he "really gets into it," it will get into him!

Lastly, be assured that, whether scripture is "straight from the Bible" or paraphrased into KIDS' language, it is God's Word, and God's Word works!

365 KIDS' CONFESSIONS

The Story of the Bible

God made the earth for people to enjoy. He wanted it to be a good and perfect and beautiful place for His people to live. He wanted to be a loving Father to every person. But the people that God made sinned. When they chose to obey the devil, they let trouble come into the earth.

God is a good God! But the devil is a bad devil. The devil brought sin, sickness, poverty, and pain into the earth. Every evil thing is from the devil.

God's heart was broken. But, because He loved His people so much, He had a plan.

Jesus, God's Son, lived with Him in Heaven. All things that were made were spoken into being by Jesus. Jesus loved the people that He and His Father God had made.

The plan was: God would let Jesus come to earth and live as a man. He would show the people how much God loved them.

Then Jesus would have to die. He would take all the sins and all the sicknesses and sorrows of the people upon Himself.

When Jesus died on the cross, for a little while the devil thought he had won. But God had a BIG surprise for him!

God raised Jesus from the dead! He was alive again! The devil's plan was defeated! Through Jesus dying and rising again, God could get His people back!

Now God's people could have power over the devil again. All they needed to do was accept Jesus as Lord and use His Word and His Name to overcome the devil!

There was hope again for the people of God! They could have a victorious life on earth and an eternal life with God and Jesus! God would be the Father He had planned to be. And we—those who believe—would be His children!

This is the story of the Bible. This is the story of God's love for mankind.

1

All your children shall be taught by the Lord,
and great shall be the peace of your children.
Isaiah 54:13

I am a child of God!
I am taught by God's Word.
I KEEP His Word in my heart!
The Word of God GUIDES my life.
I am HAPPY and BLESSED!
I have no cares, no fears, and no worries.
I am full of GOD'S PEACE.
God's Word is doing great things in my life!

2

. . . that you may become blameless and harmless, children
of God without fault in the midst of a crooked and perverse
generation, among whom you shine as lights in the world.
Philippians 2:15

Jesus is my LIGHT and His light is in me!
I will live my life as a child of God should live.
I will remember that Jesus needs me!
I am an EXAMPLE of HIS goodness and love.
I AM A LIGHT THAT SHINES even when darkness is around.
People will see my light and be led to Jesus!

3

"Let the little children come to Me, and do not forbid them;
for of such is the kingdom of God." And He took them up in
His arms, put His hands on them, and blessed them.

Mark 10:14,16

Jesus, Your Word tells me how much You love me!
You WANTED little children to come to You!
You didn't push them away. You hugged and blessed them!
I'm so glad You love me, Lord!
I FEEL YOUR PRESENCE! I FEEL YOUR LOVE!
I know I can always trust You!
I LOVE YOU, JESUS!

4

I will praise You, for I am fearfully and wonderfully made.

Psalm 139:14

Thank you, Father, for the BODY You gave me.
Thank You for making me just the way I am!
I'll take GOOD CARE of my body. I'll eat good foods,
dress wisely, exercise diligently, and rest properly.
In Jesus' Name I resist anything that would hurt my body!
Thank You, Father, for Your wisdom and Your protection
for the body I live in!

5

For whom He foreknew, He also predestinated
to be conformed to the image of His Son, that He might be
the firstborn among many brethren.
Romans 8:29

God has a SPECIAL calling on my life!
Before I was born, God knew I would want to serve Him!
I ACCEPT GOD'S CALLING. I will obey the Lord!
My life will bring glory to the Name of Jesus!
I choose to walk in God's perfect will.
I will be faithful to the trust HE has in ME!

6

Rejoice in the Lord always. Again I will say, rejoice!
Philippians 4:4

JESUS MAKES ME GLAD!
Every day I am full of JOY and STRENGTH!
I praise God in the morning!
I sing songs to Him!
I let Him know I love Him!
When night comes, I am full of peace.
I dream happy dreams!
I don't let sadness come into my heart.
I am happy, happy, happy in my Lord!

7

There is therefore now no condemnation to
those who are in Christ Jesus, who do not walk according to
the flesh, but according to the Spirit.
Romans 8:1

Father, it's so good to know that I AM YOUR CHILD!
You ALWAYS love me! Even when I sin, You love me.
The devil makes me feel guilty and bad.
But You forgive me and make me feel glad!
Nothing can ever separate me from Your love!
I'm growing STRONG in my spirit!
I'll keep right on serving You, in Jesus' Name!

8

He who is slow to wrath has great understanding.
Proverbs 14:29

I am not a pouter!
The peace of God's Spirit is in me.
I keep my temper under control!
I am kind. I am loving. I am understanding!
If I do get angry, I get over it QUICKLY!
I FORGIVE AND FORGET wrongs done to me.
I'm learning to think like Jesus!
I walk in the love of Jesus!

9

I will delight myself in Your statutes;
I will not forget Your Word.
Psalm 119:16

I'm learning MORE OF GOD'S WORD each day!
I read my Bible or listen to others read to me.
God's Word is shaping my life!
I will USE God's Word to make friends.
His Word will SHOW me how to treat others.
His Word will help me to make
EVERY DAY A DAY OF BLESSINGS!

10

(If) you pay attention to the one wearing the fine
clothes and say to him, ''You sit here in a good place,'' and
say to the poor man, ''You stand there,'' . . . have you not
shown partiality among yourselves . . .
James 2:3,4

Sometimes a new child comes into our neigborhood, school,
or church. They may feel lonely or left out.
I won't mind if the new person is rich or poor.
It doesn't matter what they wear.
I don't care what color their skin is.
The most important thing is, do they know Jesus?
I will SHOW THEM GOD'S LOVE.

11

And Jesus, when He came out, saw a great multitude
and was moved with compassion for them, because they were
like sheep not having a shepherd . . .

Mark 6:34

Jesus loves ME so much that I want to be like HIM!
I want to love EVERYONE like Jesus does!
His compassion will guide me.
I can help spread the Gospel!
I will tell the lost sheep of the world
that JESUS IS THE GOOD SHEPHERD!

12

. . . that you would have a walk worthy of God
who calls you into His own kingdom and glory.

I Thessalonians 2:12

My life is an example to others!
Others need to know what God can do FOR THEM.
They will know by seeing what God has done FOR ME.
God has made me happy!
I am victorious over the devil!
I feel IMPORTANT and LOVED.
All of my needs are met!
Because of Jesus, I have a life that
will lead others into God's Kingdom!

13

Children, obey your parents in the Lord, for this is right. ''Honor your father and mother,'' which is the first commandment with promise: ''that it may be well with you and you may live long on the earth.''

Ephesians 6:1-3

Thank You, Jesus, for my parents!
I LOVE and RESPECT my parents.
I listen to their advice.
I cheerfully do the jobs they ask me to do!
I will do my best to give my parents joy.
God will notice and will bless me.
I will always give honor to my parents!

14

Happy are the people whose God is the Lord!

Psalm 144:15b

Lord, YOU ARE MY GOD! Your power is awesome!
You're MIGHTIER than a volcano!
You are BIGGER than the ocean!
You are EVERYWHERE at once, yet always with me!
I love You! I love You! I love You!
All of my trust is in You. Trusting You keeps me HAPPY!

15

Rebuke a wise man, and he will love you.
Give instruction to a wise man, and he will be still wiser;
teach a just man, and he will increase in learning.

Proverbs 9:8,9

I'm growing in WISDOM. I want to keep LEARNING!
When I do something wrong, I'll try to make it right.
I will listen to my parents when they correct me.
I won't talk back or be angry with them.
I have a teachable spirit!
I know my life is happier when I obey!
Thank You, Lord, for parents who love and correct me.

16

Is anyone among you suffering? Let him pray. Is
anyone cheerful? Let him sing psalms.

James 5:13

I will be aware of other people's feelings.
If someone is sad, God will help me cheer them up.
I'll give them a big smile or a hug.
I'll tell them Jesus loves them!
If something is wrong, I'll pray for them.
I will be SENSITIVE to others, so
God can use ME to bless them!

17

Does a spring send forth fresh water and bitter
from the same opening?

James 3:11

The words of my mouth will be sweet.
God hears EVERYTHING I say!
I don't want to say anything that would make God sad.
Love and kindness will guide me when I speak to others.
My family, my friends, my teachers will all be
BLESSED with the words that come from my mouth!

18

Jesus said to him, ''Thomas, because you have
seen Me, you have believed. Blessed are those who
have not seen and yet have believed.''

John 20:29

I am BLESSED! JESUS IS MY LORD!
I can't see Jesus with my eyes, but
I can feel His love in my heart!
I see all the wonderful things He does!
One day I WILL see Jesus, face to face!
I'll run up to Him and give Him the
BIGGEST hug you ever saw!
I LOVE YOU, JESUS!

19

"Take heed that you do not despise one of these little ones,
for I say to you that in heaven their angels always see
the face of My Father who is in heaven."

Matthew 18:10

Angels are God's MIGHTY servants.
They travel to and from Heaven and earth.
They are sent to protect GOD'S PEOPLE!
Children have guardian angels
that watch over them all their lives.
WHEN I PRAY TO GOD, AND SPEAK GOD'S WORD
IN FAITH, THE ANGELS GET BUSY!
They see to it that the Word of God is performed!
Thank You, Lord, for Your Power, Your Word,
and Your angels watching over me!

20

But whoever listens to me will dwell safely, and will
be secure, without fear of evil.

Proverbs 1:33

Thank You, Lord, that You are always with me.
I AM NEVER ALONE.
I walk with You and talk with You.
In Your presence I have no fear!
No evil can overtake me, in Jesus' Name!

21

And whatever we ask we receive from Him,
because we keep His commandments and do those things
that are pleasing in His sight.

I John 3:22

God hears my prayers!
He is always listening to me!
He hears me because I am
His very own child.
He answers my prayers because
I am not selfish when I pray.
When I obey his commandments,
He is pleased to give
me the desires of my heart.

22

The steps of a good man are ordered by the Lord,
and He delights in his way. The law of his God is in his
heart; none of his steps shall slide.

Psalm 37:23,31

My steps are ordered by the Lord!
God will guide me all the days of my life.
The Lord will lead me to the right places
at the right times. He will give me godly friends.
God will lead me to the right person to marry.
I choose to follow Jesus! He will show me
God's perfect plan for my life!

23

"Whoever comes to Me, and hears my sayings
and does them . . . is like a man building a house, who dug
deep and laid the foundation on the rock."

Luke 6:47

I'm building my house on solid rock!
I'm digging deep into GOD'S WORD.
God's Word is Rock that can't be moved!
No matter what happens—
floods, winds, earthquakes, evils in the world—
Nothing can shake my faith in God's Word!
God's Word will remain forever!
His Truth will be my strength and my victory!

24

Sing praises to the Lord, who dwells in Zion!
Declare His deeds among the people.

Psalm 9:11

Lord Jesus,
I will sing praises to You forever!
You are my super good Friend!
You give me joy, joy, joy in my heart!
You fill me with your wisdom and knowledge.
You turn my problems into victories!
I worship and adore You, Jesus.

25

So let each one give as he purposes in his heart, not
grudgingly or of necessity; for God loves a cheerful giver.

II Corinthians 9:7

I am a cheerful giver! I am not selfish!
My money, my clothes, my toys are all from God.
I'm thankful for all the nice things I have!
God has blessed me, so I love to bless others!
Sharing my blessings shows people that God
cares about them. I become God's HELPER!
My heart delights in giving!

26   Let another man praise you, and not your own mouth . . .
Proverbs 27:2

God made me special. There's just one me!
He gave me gifts and talents and abilities.
I can be a blessing to many people!
I give thanks and honor to God for my talents!
All that I have comes from Him!
I'll not be proud or brag about what I can do.
I'll remember that God expects me to bless others
with the blessings He has given me!

27   Finally, my brethren, be strong in the Lord and in the
power of His might. Put on the whole armor of God, that you
may be able to stand against the wiles of the devil.
Ephesians 6:10,11

I begin each day putting on my ARMOR OF GOD!
When I'm wearing God's clothes,
I know I'll have a great day!
The devil will be scared to pieces!
He may try to put up a fight . . . But!
I'll just keep standing tall in God's armor
UNTIL I WIN!

28

Ephesians 6:13-18 (Personalized)

This is the armor of God I wear!
The HELMET OF SALVATION covers my head.
It protects my mind from confusion.
The BREASTPLATE OF RIGHTEOUSNESS covers my heart.
Because of Jesus shedding His blood for me,
I am holy to God.
The BELT OF TRUTH is around my waist.
My life is guided by God's truth!
GOSPEL SHOES are on my feet!
Everywhere I go, I tell God's GOOD NEWS!
I carry the SHIELD OF FAITH in my hand.
My faith causes God's Word to work . . .
My faith puts the devil on the run!
The SWORD OF THE SPIRIT is in my other hand.
The mighty Word of God cuts through every problem!
I keep my armor polished and shining with PRAYER!
Prayer surrounds myself and others with God's
POWER all through the day!

29

"And whenever you stand praying, if you have
anything against anyone, forgive him that your Father in
heaven may also forgive you your trespasses."
Mark 11:25

I am a forgiver!
Someone I love may yell at me, but I'll understand
that they didn't mean to. I'll forgive.
A friend of mine may hurt my feelings.
But I'll walk in love. I'll forgive.
Right now, I make a decision, to
forgive any wrong that has ever been done to me.
I receive total healing of all hurt.
I will always strive to be slow to get angry
and quick to forgive!

30

If there is any virtue and if there is
anything praiseworthy—meditate on these things.
Philippians 4:8

Jesus, I need Your help to stay pure.
Some music is not good for my ears to hear.
Many movies and TV shows shouldn't be seen by God's kids.
Help me to be wise! Make me strong so I can say NO
to anything that's not good in Your sight. With Your
help, I choose what is good and resist what is bad!

31 All Scripture is given by inspiration of God, and is profitable for doctrine, for reproof, for correction, for instruction in righteousness, that the man of God may be complete, thoroughly equipped for every good work.

II Timothy 3:16,17

I am equipped for every good work!
God's Word is teaching me everything I need
to know to be a soldier in His Army.
I have the Spirit of God in me!
I have God's armor on!
I have guardian angels surrounding me!
I have God's ability
growing on the inside of me!
I pray, speak, and live in God's Grace,
God's Love, and God's Authority.
He has equipped me to win!

32 When you lie down, you will not be afraid;
yes, you will lie down and your sleep will be sweet.
Proverbs 3:24

Now I lay me down to sleep . . .
And when I dream, they'll all be sweet!
Thank You, Jesus, for good, peaceful rest at night.
Thank You that you are always awake, watching over me.
Thank You for my guardian angel protecting me.
I am never afraid.
I don't mind the dark.
There's nothing to be afraid of
since You're around!
So-o-o-o,
I will close my eyes
and have happy dreams.
Good night, Jesus.
I love you.

33

Giving thanks always for all things to God the Father in
the name of our Lord Jesus Christ.
Ephesians 5:20

Father,
Thank You, Thank You, Thank You
for all the wonderful things You give me!
You fill me up with JOY!
I have no fear because You give me FAITH!
You've given me a nice, safe place to live.
I have a family to love me.
ALL my needs are met!
I appreciate Your goodness to me.
Thank You, Heavenly Father!

34

Be anxious for nothing, but in everything
by prayer and supplication, with thanksgiving,
let your requests be made known to God.
Philippians 4:6

I resist the spirit of WORRY in Jesus' Name!
I have no cares! I am GOD'S child! He meets my needs!
He keeps me safe. I am blessed in all I do.
When I pray, God hears my prayers.
I thank God always, because He never lets me down!

35

He who guards his mouth preserves his life . . . A
righteous man hates lying.

Proverbs 13:3,5a

I will guard my mouth.
I hate lies; so I don't tell them!
Lord, You always tell the truth, so I trust and believe You.
Because I tell the truth, people will trust and believe me.
In Jesus' Name, I resist temptations to lie!
I receive God's quality of Truthfulness in my life.

36

Let your gentleness be known to all men.

Philippians 4:5

Lord, You are gentle and kind.
You live in me, so I am gentle and kind, too.
I watch out for children who are smaller than me.
I am thoughtful of my classmates at school.
I speak cheerful and uplifting words.
I am polite and helpful to older people.
By my gentleness I show others the Love of God.

37

> Let us not become conceited,
> provoking one another, envying one another.
> *Galatians 5:26*

I am not proud or conceited.
I have a humble spirit.
My ways are gentle.
I do not criticize others.
I'm not bossy!
I don't cause others to get angry with me.
I show God's love to everyone.
I am always ready to be a true friend.

38

> For your obedience has become known to all.
> *Romans 16:19*

Lord,
I know YOU are watching me all the time.
The Bible says PEOPLE are watching me, too!
People around me will see JESUS in me.
They will see that I OBEY You.
They will see me LISTENING to my parents and teachers.
Because I obey, I am a GOOD example to others!
Thank You, Holy Spirit, for HELPING me to obey!

39

If you are reproached for the name of Christ, blessed are you, for the Spirit of glory and of God rests upon you . . .

I Peter 4:14

If anyone rejects me
because I love Jesus,
I'll still be happy.
I'll stand up for my Lord!
People who think they don't need Jesus will find out
that living for the devil just makes them a loser.
When they decide they want to be a winner,
I'll have the answer for them: J E S U S!

40

Behold what manner of love the Father has bestowed on us, that we should be called children of God!

I John 3:1

Father,
What love You have for me!
Because I accepted Your Son, Jesus,
You accepted me as Your child!
You became my very own Father!
You love me just the same as You love Jesus!
I will never have anything to worry about, because the God of Heaven and earth is MY FATHER!

41   Let nothing be done through selfish ambition or conceit,
but in lowliness of mind let each esteem others better than himself.
Philippians 2:3

I set a goal
to love others as much as I love myself!
I will try to think how other people feel.
I won't criticize or make fun of anyone.
God made us all. He loves each of us the same.
He wants everyone to get along with each other.
I will do my best to look through God's eyes,
and see every person as valuable and precious.

42   ''You shall rise before the gray headed and honor the
presence of an old man and fear your God: I am the Lord.''
Leviticus 19:32

God is pleased because I respect my elders.
I am polite to grownups. I say ''Yes, Sir'' and ''Yes, Ma'am.''
I am courteous. I open doors for older people.
I pick up things they drop.
I listen to the wisdom that older people have.
I don't interrupt. I'm patient and quiet.
I learn a lot from those who know more than I do.
Thank You, Lord, for putting wonderful grownups
into my life to teach me.

43

> "In my Father's house are many mansions; if it were not so,
> I would have told you. I go to prepare a place for you."
>
> *John 14:2*

I have a home in Heaven! My Heavenly Father is rich!
He has many mansions, and Jesus is preparing one for me!
I am here on earth because I have a job to do for God.
I'm helping others to learn about Jesus so they can
be children of God, too!
One day, when our work here is all finished,
we'll all take a trip to our FOREVER-HOME in Heaven!

44

> . . . he who turns a sinner from the error of his way will save
> a soul from death and cover a multitude of sins.
>
> *James 5:20*

God has given me the Words of Life.
He has put His Spirit in my heart. He has given me the tools
to save people's souls from eternal death.
I will share God's goodness!
I will use the opportunities He gives me.
When people around me sin, I won't point AT them:
I will point them TO Jesus!
I'll tell them God can make them brand new!
I'll share the love that will never fail.

45

And now abide faith, hope, love, these three;
but the greatest of these is love.

I Corinthians 13:13

The Love of God rules my life.
I walk in love towards all people.
I am very patient and kind.
I am not selfish.
I do not want what doesn't belong to me.
I am polite. I think of others first.
I am not bossy, or sassy.
I look for good things in other people.
I control my temper.
I am truthful.
My love walk will bring me friends that are faithful.
My love will draw others to the love of God.

46

I will sing to the Lord as long as I live;
I will sing praise to my God while I have my being.

Psalm 104:33

Lord,
Your love is so BIG it can't be measured!
Your goodness reaches beyond my imagination!
I love to think about You and Your kindness.
I will sing to You as long as I live.
I have a happy, happy heart!
My feet feel like dancing with joy!
I'll praise and worship and adore You forever!

47

And whatever you do, do it heartily as to the
Lord and not to men.

Colossians 3:23

I will have joy in whatever I do!
Whether I work, or whether I play,
I will make it a happy day!
I will do my best, and enjoy every task I have.
I give thanks to God for my opportunities.
The more I serve God and serve others,
the more responsibilities God will give me.
I make up my mind to please God first in all I do!

48   . . . And we knelt down on the shore and prayed.

Acts 21:5

Father,
I know praying is just TALKING TO YOU.
I can talk to You any time, anywhere, any position.
I talk to You sometimes while lying in bed.
I talk to You sitting, or standing,
or even when I'm taking a walk!
Sometimes I kneel down and just worship You.
When I worship You, I can feel Your presence
all around me.
I love You.

49   Let us draw near with a true heart in full
assurance of faith . . . Let us hold fast the confession of our
hope without wavering, for He who promised is faithful.

Hebrews 10:22a,23

My faith does not waver.
I don't allow doubt in my heart!
God is ALL GOODNESS, ALL LOVE, ALL POWER.
His nature is kindness and mercy.
His Word is truthful and sure.
I believe God with a true heart, full of faith!
I depend on God's power ALL THE TIME.
He is faithful. He helps me in all things!

50

> They desired only that we should remember
> the poor, the very thing which I also was eager to do.
> *Galatians 2:10*

I will remember the poor. I am eager to help!
Some people are poor because they don't have
enough money to buy good food or clothes.
Some people are spiritually poor because they
haven't heard the Good News about Jesus' Love.
I will do what I can to help both kinds of poor people!
The compassion of Jesus will flow through me
to help change their lives.

51

> Is anyone cheerful? Let him sing psalms.
> *James 5:13b*

I've got God's joy, joy, joy, down in my heart!
My face knows it, and my smile shows it!
I will sing praises to my God!
He is my Heavenly Father!
Jesus is my very best Friend!
The Holy Spirit is my faithful Helper!
Father, Son, and Holy Spirit
are ALL on my side! HALLELUJAH!

52 My son, give attention to my words; incline your ear to my sayings. Do not let them depart from your eyes; keep them in the midst of your heart; for they are life to those who find them, and health to all their flesh.

Proverbs 4:20-22

I pay ATTENTION to God's Word!
I KEEP God's Word in my heart!
The Words of the Lord are truthful and pure.
They will bring me long life and good health.
They will bring me success in all I do!
Thank You, Lord for the power, and
the promises, and the direction
that You give me in Your Word!

53 Therefore, as we have opportunity, let us do good to all, especially to those who are of the household of faith.

Galatians 6:10

Everyone who loves Jesus is a child of God.
I'm a member of a B-I-G family!
I have brothers and sisters all over the world!
I have a RESPONSIBILITY toward my brothers and sisters.
I will love them. I will encourage them.
I will pray for them. They are praying for me, too!
WE ALL NEED EACH OTHER!

54

Your eyes saw my substance being yet unformed.
And in Your book they all were written, the days fashioned
for me, when as yet there were none of them.

Psalm 139:16

Father, it makes me feel good to know that You saw me even
before I was born! You have a plan for my life!
I will do all I can to walk in Your plan. I know
YOU HAVE A SPECIAL JOB FOR ME TO DO.
I'm ready to get started! I'm not too young!
Thank You, Lord, that You are always ready to help me.
Together, we will get the job done!

55

Now thanks be to God who always leads us
in triumph in Christ . . .

II Corinthians 2:14

Thank You, Jesus!
With Your spirit inside of me,
there is no problem too big for us!
You and I together can handle anything!
Problems are under my feet.
The devil's tricks are under my feet!
I will be victorious in all situations
because GOD MADE ME TO WIN!

56   "I am the good shepherd; and I know My sheep,
and am known by My own."
John 10:14

Dear Jesus,
You are like a shepherd to me.
I am like Your little lamb.
I always feel safe and protected.
You watch over me day and night.
I recognize when the devil tries to talk to me.
He tells me to do things that are bad for me.
But You lead me in paths of goodness and joy.
I will listen to YOUR voice, because I trust You.

57   But as He who called you is holy, you also be holy in
all your conduct. Knowing that (you were redeemed) with
the precious blood of Christ.
I Peter 15,19

I am redeemed by the precious blood of Christ.
Jesus is my Savior and Messiah.
HE lived on earth to show ME how to live.
He DIED so I could LIVE forever.
He ROSE from the dead, so I could RISE
above the evils of the world.
His gifts to me are more precious than gold.
Jesus has made me HOLY.
I will live a holy life to honor Him!

58

There is no want to those who fear Him . . . those who
seek the Lord shall not lack any good thing.

Psalm 34:9,10

Lord, I will seek You first!
My heart will be true to You.
I will always remember Your love for me.
I will never lack any good thing . . .
For You provide all my needs.
Thank You, Lord.

59

"Be strong and of good courage . . . The Lord, He is the one who
goes before you. He will be with you. He will not leave you
nor forsake you; do not fear nor be dismayed."

Deuteronomy 31:7,8

I am strong and of good courage.
I have an important job to do in these last days.
God needs me. For the world is full of evil.
I can teach others how to overcome the world.
Wars and floods and earthquakes shake the earth.
But evil will not overtake me!
Fear will not come into my heart.
The Lord my God is with me!
In all I do, He will help me.
He gives me grace and strength and courage.
I will be true to my God and He will be true to me.

For Leap Year or Any Year!

"Do not lay up for yourselves treasures on earth, where moth
and rust destroy and where thieves break in and steal: but
lay up for yourselves treasures in heaven . . . for where your
treasure is, there your heart will be also."
Matthew 6:19,20b,2l

God owns the whole earth!
God will see to it that I have all I need!
I won't worry about storing up earthly treasures.
I will use my energy to store up treasures in Heaven!
When I lead someone to Jesus, that is treasure in Heaven.
When I give to the needy, I receive treasure in Heaven.
When I pray for the sick, and cheer up the brokenhearted,
I'm storing up treasures in Heaven.

When I stand up for Jesus,
And give honor to His Name,
Great will be my reward in Heaven!

60

Listen to your father who begot you, and do not
despise your mother when she is old.

Proverbs 23:22

Thank You for my parents, Lord.
I appreciate all my Mom and Dad do for me.
I will listen to their advice.
I'll obey when they ask me to do—
or not to do—something!
I'll always tell them the truth.
I'll help them as much as I can.
I will be a blessing to them all the days of their life!

61

For do I now persuade men, or God?
Or do I seek to please men? For if I still pleased men,
I would not be a servant of Christ.

Galatians 1:10

I live my life to please God!
God is my boss! His Word is my teacher!
I will tell the truth of God's Word everywhere.
Some people don't want to hear the truth.
But I'll walk in love and tell them the truth anyway!
God will be pleased with me,
because I'll be doing what He said!

62

My little children, these things I write to you, that you may not sin . . . (But if we do sin), He is faithful and just to forgive us our sins and to cleanse us from all unrighteousness.

I John 2:1, 1:9

I don't want to sin!
I resist the devil and any ideas he might give me!
Jesus, You are helping me not to sin.
Your Word and Your Spirit guide me.
But if I do make a bad choice and sin,
I'll come running TO YOU.
You'll know I'm really sorry, and You'll forgive me.
Thank You, Jesus, that I can always come to You!

63

But let all those rejoice who put their trust in You.

Psalm 5:11

Father, I put my faith in You.
Your Words will never fail.
Your love will never let me down!
I trust You with everything that concerns me.
I know YOU CARE about anything I care about!
I will rejoice because I'm in Your hands!

64

Be of good comfort, be of one mind, live in peace; and
the God of love and peace will be with you.

II Corinthians 3:11b

I can help make my home one of peace and love!
I will be in agreement with my parents.
I'll get along with my brother(s) and sister(s).
I resist strife!
I will stop arguments before they start!
I'll give comfort to anyone in my family who is upset.
Our home will be filled with love, in Jesus' Name.

65

These . . . things the Lord hates . . . a proud look,
a lying tongue . . . a false witness who speaks lies,
and one who sows discord among brethren.

Proverbs 6:16,17,19

Lord, I want to please You in all I do.
I don't want to do anything to make You sad.
The Bible says You hate lying.
Help me to always be truthful.
Help me to be honest with You and with others.
I want people to believe me when I say something.
They will trust me, because they'll know I don't lie!

66

So (Paul and Silas) said, "Believe on the Lord Jesus
Christ, and you will be saved, you and your household."
Acts 16:31

Jesus, I believe on You. You are my Lord and Savior.
You love me, my parents, and our whole family.
I stand on Your Word and ask that Your Spirit work in
every member of my family!
If there are any who do not know You,
I pray that they will receive You.
Send people to them to share Your love.
I claim and believe that ALL of my family, near or far,
will be born again!
In the name of Jesus, Amen!

67

But let him ask in faith, with no doubting, for he who doubts
is like a wave of the sea driven and tossed by the wind.
James 1:6

Father,
Thank You for Your wisdom working in me!
I'm becoming STRONG in Your Word! I'm growing every day
in knowledge of You. I resist doubt and unbelief!
I walk by faith! The wisdom of God is shaping what I
desire, what I think about, and what I do! Hallelujah!

68

Praise the Lord!
Psalm 148:1

Praise the Lord, all of Heaven!
Praise the Lord in the earth below!
Praise the Lord, all you mighty angels!
Praise Him, sun, moon, and stars!
Praise the Lord, little children!
Praise the Lord, fathers and mothers!
Let all people praise the Name of the Lord!
Unto Him is all Honor and Power and Glory forever!

69

Make no friendship with an angry man,
and with a furious man do not go, lest you learn
his ways and set a snare for your soul.
Proverbs 22:24,25

I am careful who I choose for my friends. I trust God to
send me godly friends at every age of my life.
He will give me friends who love and accept me.
He will send friends who are faithful and encouraging.
God will lead me to friends who are a good example.
I will BE a good friend to those the Lord sends me.
I will be someone they can depend on.

70

Then Peter said to them . . . "you shall receive the gift of the Holy Spirit. For the promise is to you and to your children, and to all who are afar off, as many as the Lord our God shall call."

Acts 2:38,39

Thank You, Lord, that You saw ME 2000 years ago, when You promised Your people would be filled with the Holy Spirit!
You knew I would need extra POWER to live a happy life!
Thank You, Holy Spirit, for working mightily in me!
I am a member of God's Power Team! With You as my coach, even if troubles come, we'll stay in the game until we win!

71

"But the Helper, the Holy Spirit, whom the Father will send in My name, He will teach you all things, and bring to your remembrance all things that I said to you."

John 14:26

Thank You, Holy Spirit, for being my Helper.
You are my Teacher. You help me to understand God's Word.
You show me how to know right from wrong.
You help me to remember the things Jesus wants me to know.
You're always aware of when I need Your help.
I depend on You, Holy Spirit.
I appreciate You!

72

For He Himself has said, "I will never leave you
nor forsake you." So we may boldly say: "The Lord is my
helper; I will not fear. What can man do to me?"

Hebrews 13:5b,6

Jesus said He would never leave me nor forsake me.
He is always near because His Spirit is in me!
No matter what evils are in the world around me,
God is in the middle of me! He will not fail me!
I have no fear! I will rest in
peace at night and walk in faith by day.
THE LORD, MY GOD IS WITH ME!

73

You have put gladness in my heart!

Psalm 4:7

Lord Jesus,
Your love makes me feel good all over!
I can't be sad when I'm thinking of You.
You take such good care of me I can't worry!
You help me solve all my problems.
You give me joy inside that nothing can take away!
I'm so happy I have to spread it all over the place!
Hallelujah!

74

Your hands have made me and fashioned me;
give me understanding, that I may learn your commandments.
Psalm 119:73

God made me!
He saw me before I was born!
There is no one else just like me!
The God who made me will guide my steps.
He will help me make good choices, wise decisions.
His Spirit will help me to fulfill His will in all I do.

75

For the eyes of the Lord are on the
righteous, and his ears are open to their prayers.
I Peter 3:12

Lord, You are always listening to me.
You hear me no matter how I talk to You.
Sometimes I talk LOUD to You.
Sometimes I WHISPER.
Even when I pray in my heart, You still hear me.
You are God, and You know what I'm going to
say even before I say it!
It doesn't matter how I pray, or when, or where—
You ALWAYS hear; You always care!

76   Blessings are on the head of the righteous.
Proverbs 10:6

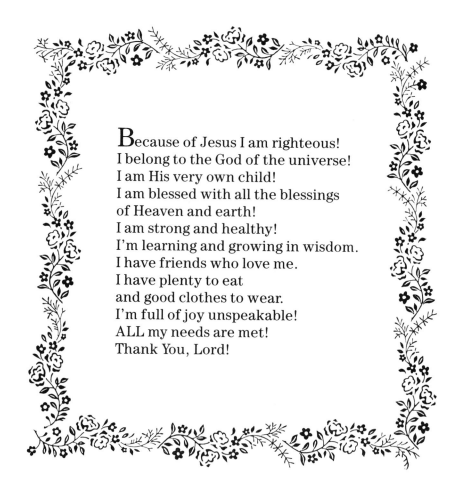

Because of Jesus I am righteous!
I belong to the God of the universe!
I am His very own child!
I am blessed with all the blessings
of Heaven and earth!
I am strong and healthy!
I'm learning and growing in wisdom.
I have friends who love me.
I have plenty to eat
and good clothes to wear.
I'm full of joy unspeakable!
ALL my needs are met!
Thank You, Lord!

77

A wholesome tongue is a tree of life.
Proverbs 15:4a

I put a guard on my lips!
I'm careful what I listen to and what I say.
I don't stay around people who say bad words.
I won't listen to gossip about other people.
I want to live a happy, healthy, long life.
So my words are pure, kind, and uplifting!

78

A merry heart makes a cheerful countenance, but by
sorrow of the heart the spirit is broken.
Proverbs 15:13

I love to be around people who are cheerful!
So, I will be cheerful, too!
Then people will love to be around ME!
Because I make them happy!
I'm not a pouter . . . No, sir! I'm a smiler!
I'm not sad . . . I'm happy! I'm not mad . . . I'm glad!
Happiness shows all over me,
because the Lord's joy is in my heart!

79
For I am not ashamed of the gospel of Christ, for it is the
power of God to salvation for everyone who believes . . .
Romans 1:16

The Gospel is GOD'S GOOD NEWS!
The Gospel is Jesus coming to earth to save me!
God let Jesus come to die for my sins.
But the GOOD news is that Jesus rose up again!
He whipped the devil! He did it so I could be
saved from the devil running my life!
I don't have to be sick, poor, or defeated!
I am a winner because of God's Good News!

80
But without faith it is impossible to please Him, for
he who comes to God must believe that He is, and that He is
a rewarder of those who diligently seek Him.
Hebrews 11:6

God is happy when I use my faith!
FAITH simply means I BELIEVE GOD.
Faith says, "I believe God's Word is true,
and I depend on it." Faith says, "God is good!
He has rewards for me when I put Him first!"
Thank You, Lord, for helping me to grow STRONG IN FAITH!

81   The plans of the diligent lead surely to plenty.
Proverbs 21:5

If I work hard, I can get lots more things done.
I can help Mom and Dad and still have time to play!
I can work hard at school lessons, and learn
things that will help me all my life!
I can work diligently in God's Word
and do my part to change the world!
I'm a worker and not a loafer, in Jesus' Name!

82   He sent His Word and healed them.
Psalm 107:20

There is healing in God's Word.
When I speak God's Word, I grow stronger.
When I hear God's Word, sickness has to flee.
Disease and infection run out the door!
Health comes! Because God's Word works in my body!
I walk in health and strength, in Jesus' Name!

83

Be sober, be vigilant; because your adversary the
devil walks about like a roaring lion, seeking whom he may
devour. Resist him, steadfast in the faith!

I Peter 5:8,9

God is on my side! God has an enemy named Satan.
Because I belong to God, Satan is my enemy, too.
The devil looks for ways to bring trouble to me.
But I resist him!
I have extra power from God's Holy Spirit!
God's ability is on the inside of me!
God and I together will put the enemy on the run!

84

The angel of the Lord encamps
all around those who fear Him, and delivers them.

Psalm 34:7

Heavenly Father,
Thank You for putting angels all around me.
I can't see the angels with my natural eyes,
but Your Word says they are watching over me.
They have a job to do. They help You protect me!
They keep evil away from me!
I will be obedient to You, Father,
so the angels will be able to do their job!

85 Do not love the world or the things in the world. If anyone
loves the world, the love of the Father is not in him.
I John 2:15

My heart belongs to Jesus!
He is my first love!
I don't love the things of the world
or things money can buy.
I enjoy all the blessings God gives me,
but I don't live to receive . . .
I live to give.
I live to love.
My goal is to live forever with Jesus and
to show others they can, too!

86   An excellent wife is the crown of her husband.
Proverbs 12:4

I'm not too young to claim just the right person to marry.
God is already working on my future mate!
He's preparing someone wonderful to share my life.
A joyful person who loves Jesus is on the way!
We will have a loving marriage and family.
God will be the center of our home.
Thank You, Jesus, for preparing us to be together!

87   Bring all the tithes into the storehouse, that
there may be food in My house.
Malachi 3:10a

I am a tither!
I joyfully give back to God one tenth of all
the money He sends to me.
One tenth of my allowance belongs to God.
One tenth of money I earn goes back to God.
I am so blessed I want to give MORE than a tenth!
Giving to God is one way of saying
"Thank You, Father, for all You've given to me."
GIVING TO GOD TELLS HIM I LOVE HIM!

88

II Peter 1:2-8 (Personalized)

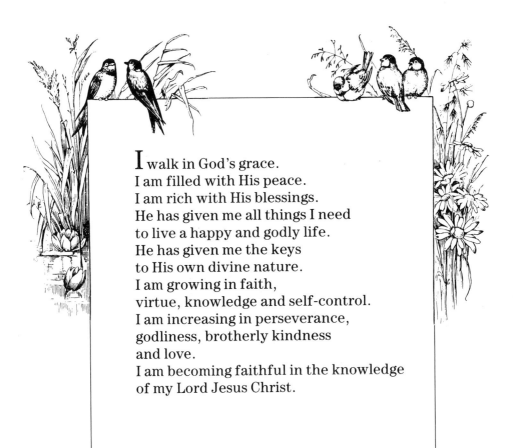

I walk in God's grace.
I am filled with His peace.
I am rich with His blessings.
He has given me all things I need
to live a happy and godly life.
He has given me the keys
to His own divine nature.
I am growing in faith,
virtue, knowledge and self-control.
I am increasing in perseverance,
godliness, brotherly kindness
and love.
I am becoming faithful in the knowledge
of my Lord Jesus Christ.

89

Beloved, let us love one another, for love is of
God; and everyone who loves is born of God and knows God.

I John 4:7

God is love!
I love God! I show that I love God
by loving other people all around me.
I love my family, my friends, my classmates.
I love people who don't even know me!
Because I walk in love, the Bible says I know God!
It's great to KNOW the one true God!
It's great to know GOD loves ME!

90

"Go home to your friends, and tell them what great
things the Lord has done for you . . . "

Mark 5:19

Lord Jesus,
You have done great things for me! I'll never forget You!
I'll constantly tell how wonderful You are.
I'll let my friends and family know how much You love us.
I'll share Your Good News with my mailman,
and grocery man, and my neighbors.
You can help anyone, Jesus, if they ask You to.
I'll let people know they can count on You!

91   Happy is the man who is always reverent.
Proverbs 28:14

Heavenly Father, You love me and
take care of me and make me feel important.
But You also expect me to obey You!
You command me to honor Your Word.
You expect me to imitate Jesus.
I know if I disobey I will not be happy.
I set my goal to always obey You, Father.
I will both love and respect You!

92   (He who delights in the Lord) shall
be like a tree planted by the rivers of water, that brings
forth its fruit in its season, whose leaf also shall not
wither; and whatever he does shall prosper.
Psalm 1:3

God's Word is GROWING on the inside of me!
I'm growing, too! I'm like a tree in God's Garden.
He is the gardener who tends me and prunes me so
I'll become a beautiful tree full of good fruit!
Anything I do that counts for good in God's Kingdom
is GOOD FRUIT. With God's help, whatever I do
will prosper and succeed!

93   ''For assuredly, I say to you, whoever says to this mountain,
'Be removed and be cast into the sea,' and does not doubt in
his heart, but believes that those things he says will come
to pass, he will have whatever he says.''

Mark 11:23

I have mountain moving faith!
The more faith I use, the more God gives me!
God and I together can handle any problem that comes.
I believe in God MORE than I believe in the problem!
Even if I think the problem is as big as a mountain,
in Jesus' Name we can move it!
Nothing will stop me from following Jesus!
Nothing will stop me from being a blessing
to God's Kingdom!

94
>Receive one who is weak in the faith,
>but not to disagree over doubtful things.
>*Romans 14:1*

If someone disagrees about my faith,
I won't argue with them. If they don't believe
God's Word the way I do, I will pray for them.
I'll keep on loving them.
They will learn more about Jesus by my love
than by arguing! I will be the example of Jesus
to them. And God will do the rest!

95
>"Greater love has no one than this,
>than to lay down one's life for his friends.
>You are my friends if you do whatever I command you."
>*John 15:13,14*

Jesus loves me so much He laid down His life for me.
He proved He wanted to be my Friend.
I will be Your friend, Jesus.
All I have is Yours. All You have is mine.
I will listen to You with great respect.
I'll honor You with my thoughts, words, and actions.
I have no friend more faithful than You!
I love You, Lord!

96   ''My sheep hear My voice, and I know them, and they follow Me.
And I give them eternal life, and they shall never perish;
neither shall anyone snatch them out of My hand.''

John 10:27,28

I follow Jesus like a little lamb follows its shepherd.
No enemy will ever steal me away from Jesus!
I KNOW my Shepherd's voice.
God's Word is one way the Shepherd talks to me.
His Holy Spirit talks to my spirit.
I have special inner ears to hear His voice.
I will listen to the Good Shepherd.
I will obey and be safe.

97   Likewise you also, reckon yourselves to be dead
indeed to sin, but alive to God in Christ Jesus our Lord.

Romans 6:11

God gives me a choice—to obey, or disobey.
I'm sorry when I disobey. I repent of those sins.
But even though I goof at times, sin is not my boss!
I'm growing in God's grace every day!
I'm learning to be the boss over the devil!
I am alive to God in Christ Jesus my Lord!
Jesus is my real boss! He's the One I want to please!

98   Being confident of this very thing, that He who has begun a
good work in you will complete it until the day of Jesus Christ.

Philippians 1:6

God has begun a good work in me!
He gave me Jesus!
He filled me with the Holy Spirit!
He's giving me understanding in His Word.
With all these gifts I am a strong Christian!
I have power to overcome any challenge!
God is helping me to walk daily in His plan!

99   . . . He guards all his bones; not one of them is broken.

Psalm 34:20

Lord, I look to You for all my help.
You are my Protector.
Mom and Dad trust You to take care of me,
and I trust You.
I won't do things that are dangerous.
I will obey Mom and Dad.
But if an accident happens,
I believe You will protect my life.
You will even protect my bones.
Thank You, Lord, for Your protection!

100

Make a joyful shout to the Lord, all you lands!
Psalm 100:1

I will shout to the Lord with joy!
I serve my Lord with gladness.
I come into His presence with singing.
I remember that God made me and I am His!
I enter His gates with thanksgiving.
I praise Him and bless His Holy Name!
For the Lord is good.
His mercy is everlasting!
His truth shall bless all generations!

101

Obey those who rule over you, and be submissive, for they watch out for your souls, as those who must give account.
Hebrews 13:17

I obey those God has placed over me. My parents.
My teachers. My pastor. All of these people have
a BIG responsibility. God told them to watch out for
my soul! God told them to teach me and train me.
I listen to my elders with respect. I learn with joy.
I have a cheerful attitude, and an obedient heart.
The angels will be keeping good heavenly records on me!

102

God is love.
I John 4:8b

God loves me! He calls me His BELOVED.
He says I am the APPLE OF HIS EYE!
He loves me with an EVERLASTING LOVE.
His love will NEVER FAIL.
He will NEVER LEAVE ME NOR FORSAKE ME.
I'm HIS LITTLE CHILD.
He's MY LOVING FATHER.
GOD'S LOVE WILL SURROUND ME FOREVER!

103

This is the day which the Lord has made;
we will rejoice and be glad in it.
Psalm 118:24

Thank You, Jesus,
for another day of Your goodness and love!
This will be a day of learning and growing.
I call this day blessed!
I will do my best to make it a happy day.
I will be glad and rejoice!
My heart will sing with joy!
I will spread joy to others all around me!

104

My son, do not forget my law, but let
your heart keep my commands; for length of days
and long life and peace they will add to you.

Proverbs 3:1,2

My Bible is a treasure that I cherish.
I love God's Word because I know He's talking to me!
I do my best to listen to God and live by His Word.
I will have a long, healthy life
because God's Word is working in me!
I'll have peace and joy no matter what,
because His Word keeps my faith strong!

105

"Peace I leave with you, My peace I give to you;
not as the world gives do I give to you. Let not your heart
be troubled, neither let it be afraid."

John 14:27

Dear Lord,
No matter what happens around me—in my family, or in
school, or in the world—I will always be filled with
Your peace. My heart will not be troubled or afraid.
You will always be able to work things out,
because my faith is working! I walk in faith, not fear!
THE PEACE YOU GIVE controls my feelings!

106 Therefore we do not lose heart. Even though our outward man
is perishing, yet the inward man is being renewed day by day.
II Corinthians 4:16

I am not discouraged. I am full of hope!
My hope is in my God! He makes all things good.
He fixes things that go wrong. My heart is full of joy
because I trust in Him. My spirit is lively and strong!
My inner man will stand up tall and shout,
"Hallelujah! Nothing can keep me down!"

107 Yet in all these things we are
more than conquerors through Him who loved us.
Romans 8:37

I am more than a conqueror!
Jesus has already won the battle against the devil.
When Jesus died, Satan couldn't hold Him down!
He rose again!
He went to Heaven and sent His power back to me!
So, Satan can't hold me down, either!
I will keep on believing God.
I will keep on trusting in His Word.
In Jesus' Name I walk in VICTORY!

108

Let each of you look out not only for his
own interests, but also for the interests of others.
Philippians 2:4

I am not in this world just for myself.
Others around need my love. Others need my smiles.
Sometimes they need a hug or a pat on the back.
I will look around and see where I can be a blessing.
I can make a difference in someone's life every day!

109

You ask and do not receive, because you ask amiss,
that you may spend it on your pleasures.
James 4:3

Lord, when I pray
Your Spirit shows me what to ask for.
I am not selfish, just praying for things I want.
My prayers are for the lives and needs of others, too.
I know that when I'm thinking of You first,
and remembering others with love,
You will give me all the things I really need.
I will receive, because I want what You want!

110
For our citizenship is in Heaven . . .
Philippians 3:20

My Father God has prepared a home for me in Heaven.
It's more gorgeous than the biggest mansion on earth!
I live in the earth now, but I'm a CITIZEN of Heaven!
I will do all I can to glorify God while I'm here.
But no matter where I am or what I'm doing,
I'll remember that my real home is waiting for me
in Heaven!

111
Let the saints be joyful in glory!
Psalm 149:5

When I get to Heaven,
I'm going to meet all of God's heroes!
I'm going to be friends with Abraham and Sarah,
Noah, Samuel, Ruth, and David . . . John, Peter, and Paul!
If Brother Enoch comes up and asks me,
''Did you read about me in the Bible?'',
I'll say, ''Yes, Sir!''
If Queen Esther asks, ''Did you read about me?'',
I'll say, ''Yes, Ma'am!''
It will really be neat! Everyone will know me
And I'll know them!

112

Therefore, if anyone is in Christ, he is a new creation; old things have passed away; behold, all things have become new.

II Corinthians 5:17

I am a spirit being.
I live in a body, but the real ME is my spirit!
When I received Jesus, my spirit was born again.
I became part of God and He became part of me.
The Power of God's Spirit is in my spirit!
The love of God is in my spirit!
My spirit can control the way I think, speak and act.
I will let God's power rule my spirit, my soul and my body!

113

You shall love the Lord your God with all your heart, with all your soul, and with all your might.

Deuteronomy 6:5

I am a spirit. The life of God is in my spirit.
My spirit will live forever!
I have a soul. My soul is my mind and my thinking.
I live in a body. My body is a house for my spirit
and my soul. I will take good care of my body
because God's Spirit lives in it like a temple.
I will protect my mind, because the way I think and believe
makes me different from those who are not Christians.
I will guard my spirit by letting Jesus
be Lord of all my life!

114

Beloved, I pray that you may prosper in all things
and be in health, just as your soul prospers.

III John 2

When I received Jesus, my spirit was made brand new,
but my soul was not. I have to train my soul!
I must feed it with the Word of God.
I must exercise it with faith, and prayer, and worship.
I must guard my thoughts and keep them pure.
I will make decisions which honor Jesus.
Every day my soul will prosper and grow stronger!

115

For you were bought at a price; therefore glorify God
in your body and in your spirit, which are God's.

I Corinthians 6:20

Jesus bought me.
He paid for my life with His own blood.
My spirit, my soul, and my body belong to God.
I will keep my body pure. No cigarettes or alcohol or
drugs will get into my body. I will stay away from
places that would harm my body. I will glorify God
in what I say, and what I do, and where I go!
I belong to JESUS!

116

Not lagging in diligence,
fervent in spirit, serving the Lord . . .
Romans 12:11

I'm a worker for the Lord! I'm not lazy!
I am diligent! At home, at school, everywhere!
I'm in training for an important job from the Lord!
I am full of energy for Jesus! I am faithful!
Jesus can count on me when He needs me!
I'm ready, willing and able to help change the world!

117

Distributing to the needs of the saints . . .
Romans 12:13

Saints are people who are doing God's work.
They need money just like we need money in my family.
They have places to go, people in need, and bills to pay.
I want to help the workers who spread the Gospel!
Whenever I get money, I will give some away to the saints.
I will help cover the world with God's Good News!

118

I will bless the Lord who has given me counsel;
my heart also instructs me in the night seasons.
Psalm 16:7

Bless You, Lord!
Your Word always tells me the right thing to do.
I always look to You first for advice.
You speak to my spirit and I know Your voice!
Even when I am asleep I hear from You.
I grow in wisdom daily as Your Word grows in me.
I make good choices because Your Holy Spirit guides me!

119

For God has not given us a spirit of fear,
but of power and of love and of a sound mind.
II Timothy 1:7

God has given me POWER!
I have authority over the devil, in Jesus' Name!
God has given me His LOVE. I have no fear of anything.
God's presence surrounds me like a wall of protection.
God has given me a SOUND MIND.
I am free from confusion, guilt, or worry.
I am full of faith and confidence!
Glory to God forever!

120

. . . rather to be absent from the
body and to be present with the Lord.

II Corinthians 5:8

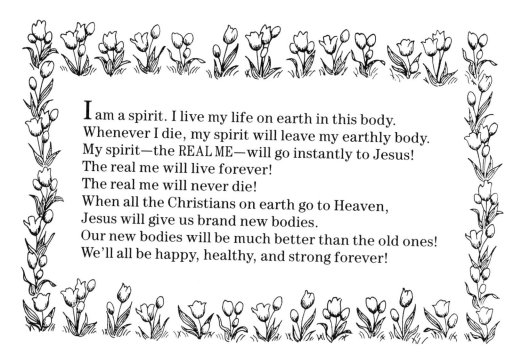

I am a spirit. I live my life on earth in this body.
Whenever I die, my spirit will leave my earthly body.
My spirit—the REAL ME—will go instantly to Jesus!
The real me will live forever!
The real me will never die!
When all the Christians on earth go to Heaven,
Jesus will give us brand new bodies.
Our new bodies will be much better than the old ones!
We'll all be happy, healthy, and strong forever!

121   And do not be conformed to this world, but be transformed
by the renewing of your mind, that you may prove what is
that good and acceptable and perfect will of God.
Romans 12:2

The Lord of creation lives in me!
My mind is renewed daily by His living Word!
I'm learning to think like Jesus thinks!
I don't have to live like the world tells people to live.
I have a better way! I'll show the world
how people who love Jesus live!
I'll prove that the best road to follow is found
on God's ROADMAP — THE BIBLE!

122   Therefore God also has highly exalted Him and
given Him the name which is above every name.
Philippians 2:11

Jesus! Jesus! Jesus! Oh, how I love Jesus!
Angels worship Him. Saints adore Him.
Demons tremble before His Name.
The Maker of heaven and earth is my Savior!
My mouth is full of His praises.
My lips sing and shout for joy!
My knees bow in worship.
For great is my wonderful Lord!

123   Now to Him who is able to do exceedingly abundantly above all
that we ask or think, according to the power that works in us . . .
Ephesians 3:20

God can do great things through me! Whenever I say
"YES!" to Him, I open the door so His Power can work!
He can use me more than I ever thought possible.
He can use my faith to move mountains.
I can pray for the sick, and bring hope to the lost.
God is able to use me because I have a willing heart,
and an obedient life!

124   Bless the Lord, you His angels, who excel in
strength who do His Word, heeding the voice of His Word.
Psalm 103:20

God has given me His Word to help me grow strong.
God is always listening to hear if I speak His Word.
He has told the angels to be listening for His Word, too.
As I SPEAK THE WORD OF GOD, the angels get busy!
They help bring about what I'm saying in faith.
Thank You, Lord, for all the ways
You help me to live in victory!

125

"I chose you and appointed you that you should go
and bear fruit, and that your fruit should remain, that
whatever you ask the Father in My name He may give you."
John 15:16

Jesus, it's AWESOME that YOU CHOSE ME!
I will do my best to live up to Your faith in me!
I'll go and bear fruit in Your Name.
The fruit You help me produce is good fruit.
It will remain. The things I do to bring honor
to You will last long after the things of the world
are gone! Thank You, Jesus, for trusting me!

126

Be of the same mind toward one another.
Romans 12:16

Through the blood of Jesus, I am a brother/sister
to all Christians in God's family.
God sees me just the same as He sees everyone else.
He loves us all the same.
He corrects and teaches each of us.
None of us is better or higher up than another.
I will look at every person through God's eyes.
Every single person is valuable and precious!

127

Ask of Me, and I will give
you the nations for your inheritance.
Psalm 2:8

I love the people of this world!
I want to be a part of what God is doing.
I spread God's love. I pray for all the people
who don't know Jesus. I ask for souls to be saved!
I claim my neighbors! I claim friends and teachers!
I'm going to be involved in worldshaking revival!
God said ask for souls and I would receive!
When I get to Heaven, I'll look around and see
PEOPLE who are there BECAUSE I HELPED!

128

Only let your conduct be worthy of the gospel of
Christ . . . stand fast in one spirit, with one mind striving
together for the faith of the gospel.
Philippians 1:27

My behavior represents the Gospel of Jesus.
For some people, the only Jesus they can imagine
is the Jesus they see in my actions.
I have a big responsibility! My words will be kind.
The way I treat others will show God's goodness.
The Light of Jesus will shine through me!

129

If a man vows a vow to the Lord, or swears an oath to bind himself by some agreement, he shall not break his word; he shall do according to all that proceeds out of his mouth.

Numbers 30:2

When I make a promise, I keep my word.
God looks at promises very seriously. He always
keeps His promises! He never changes His mind.
So, when I say I'll do something, I do it!
God's Spirit will remind me to keep my word.
God and others will know they can trust me!

130

That we should no longer be children, tossed to and fro . . . but speaking the truth in love, may grow up in all things into Him who is the head—Christ . . .

Ephesians 4:14a,15

I am growing up in the things of God.
I speak the truth! Lies have no place in me!
The devil might tempt me, but he can't make me lie!
I have control! The choice is mine!
I choose the way of Truth!
I will always be blessed by my truthfulness,
because people will know they can believe what I say!

131
> Trust in the Lord, and do good; dwell in the land,
> and feed on His faithfulness. Delight yourself also in the
> Lord, and He shall give you the desires of your heart.
> *Psalm 37:3,4*

Lord Jesus, I trust in You. I do good.
I meditate on Your Word. I think about You all day.
I delight myself in knowing You as my Friend!
You shall direct all my steps.
Serving You will give me a happy, fruitful life.
You know all the desires of my heart, and You will give
them to me in Your timing. Thank You, Jesus.

132
> But the prayer of the upright is His delight.
> *Proverbs 15:8b*

God loves to hear me pray!
He's happy when I talk to Him about just anything.
He is pleased when I pray about the needs of others.
I can talk to God anytime, day or night.
He is always listening.
God answers my prayers because I am His child!

133

I Peter 3:10-12 (Personalized)

I will see God's goodness all the days of my life!
I will keep my tongue from evil;
My lips will speak no lies.
I will not follow evil but will do good.
I will seek peace and pursue it.
For the eyes of the Lord are upon me;
His ears are open to my prayers.
He will deliver me from every trouble!

134

A merry heart does good, like medicine,
but a broken spirit dries the bones.
Proverbs 17:22

I am full of the joy of the Lord!
I have a merry heart!
I'm so happy that sadness can't come in!
Sickness runs away from me!
Trusting the Lord turns worries into joys!
Joy in my heart is like good medicine to my body!
The joy of the Lord is my strength!

135

> "See, I have set the land before you; go in and
> possess the land which the Lord swore to your fathers
> to give to them and their descendants after them."
> *Deuteronomy 1:8*

God plans for me to have an abundant life! A good home,
an education, health and safety, and a long life are mine!
But the devil doesn't want me to receive anything!
I must use God's weapons and drive off the devil!
I'll wear God's armor! I'll pray with Power!
I'll use the Sword of the Spirit on the devil!
That robber can't hold my blessings back!
I will receive all God intends for me in Jesus' Name!

136

> For we dare not class ourselves or compare ourselves with
> those who commend themselves. They . . . are not wise.
> *II Corinthians 10:12*

I don't compare myself with other people.
God has given ME special gifts and talents.
He has given OTHERS special gifts and talents.
All of our ability is FROM HIM.
I'll compare myself with what GOD expects of me.
I will work hard to do all I'm able to do
with the abilities God gave me!
That's the way I will be successful!

137   That the genuineness of your faith, being much more precious
than gold that perishes, though it is tested by fire, may be found
to praise, honor, and glory at the revelation of Jesus Christ.

I Peter 1:17

My faith is more precious than gold!
My faith assures me that I belong to Jesus!
My faith convinces me that God's promises will happen
if I don't doubt. God will test my faith.
He tests me because He wants me to grow STRONG in faith.
I will be valuable in God's Kingdom,
because my faith is always growing stronger!

138   Oh, how I love Your law!
It is my meditation all the day.

Psalm 119:97

Lord, Your Word plants Your wisdom in me.
Knowing Your Word gives me godly understanding.
Hearing Your Word increases my faith.
Your Word lightens my path and shows me which way to go.
In Your Word are the answers to all of my concerns.
Thank You, Lord, for giving me Your Word—The Bible.

139

"And when you offer a sacrifice of thanksgiving
to the Lord, offer it of your own free will."
Leviticus 22:29

I love to give to God! When I put money into church,
I'm showing the Lord that I am thankful. I'm saying that
I appreciate all the wonderful things He has given me!
My giving back to God will help get
the things done that He wants to in the earth.
Every bit that I give will be
helping someone, somewhere to know Jesus.

140

Looking for the blessed hope and glorious appearing of our
great God and Savior Jesus Christ, who gave Himself for us,
that He might redeem us from every lawless deed and purify
for Himself His own people, zealous for good works.
Titus 2:13,14

I belong to Jesus! He gave His own life to rescue ME
from the devil! I love Jesus with all my heart!
I'm excited about serving the Lord!
He's my HERO! When I see Jesus,
I'm going to give Him ten thousand hugs and kisses!
I'll worship and praise Him and dance for joy!
I love You, Jesus! I love You! I love You! I love You!

141

"However, when He, the Spirit of truth, has come,
He will guide you into all truth . . .
John 16:13

Holy Spirit, You are my Helper. I trust You.
You will guide me into all truth.
I will not be deceived by lies of the devil.
I hear Your voice in my spirit.
I'm growing sensitive in knowing Your voice,
because I test all my thoughts by God's Word.
As I listen and obey I will be mighty in the Lord!

142

And this I pray, that your love may abound
still more and more in knowledge and all discernment . . .
Philippians 1:9

Thank You, Holy Spirit, for spiritual discernment.
You help me to know in my heart what is right and wrong.
I am able to tell which people are Christlike
and which ones are only pretending.
I know who are my real friends and who are not.
I recognize plans of the devil and I resist them.
I love the things of God, and I walk in His truth!

143

Therefore, my beloved brethren, let every man be
swift to hear, slow to speak, slow to wrath; for the wrath
of man does not produce the righteousness of God.

James 1:19,20

In order to please God, I need to act like Jesus!
I'm not fussy or angry! I'm patient and peaceful!
I'm learning when to talk and when to stay quiet.
I am a good listener! I am polite.
I don't say foolish things.
My words are uplifting and encouraging.
I am swift to hear, slow to get angry,
and quick to walk in love!

144

Let no corrupt communication proceed out of your mouth,
but what is good for necessary edification,
that it may impart grace to the hearers.

Ephesians 4:29

I bless others with the words of my mouth!
I let them know they are important. I tell them they
did a nice job! I am sincere and truthful.
The words I say come from my heart.
I find something good to say about everyone.
Those who hear me will be encouraged!

145

Guard what was committed to your trust,
avoiding the profane and vain babblings and contradictions
of what is falsely called knowledge . . .
I Timothy 6:20

I will guard the treasures God has given me!
He has given me salvation: I'll walk close to Jesus!
He has given me health: I will take care of my body!
He has given me His Holy Spirit:
I will use my authority against works of darkness!
He has given me the Bible: I will use my knowledge
of His Word to live a Holy, fruitful life!

146

And let us not grow weary while doing good,
for in due season we shall reap if we do not lose heart.
Galatians 6:9

I will never get tired of serving God! People may not
understand me. Some will say I'm different. They may
even make fun of me. Well, I AM different!
I don't belong to this world! I belong to God!
When people around me have a problem,
when they are afraid or lonely, they will come to me.
They know I have the answer they need: JESUS.

147   As you have therefore received Christ Jesus the Lord, so walk
in Him, rooted and built up in Him and established in the faith . . .
Colossians 2:6, 7a

I walk in the knowledge of Christ Jesus, my Lord!
I am like a tree with STRONG ROOTS. My roots are
in Jesus, so I will grow, GROW, G-R-O-W!
I will produce good works that glorify God.
My life will make a difference in the earth!

148   What then shall we say to these things?
If God is for us, who can be against us?
Romans 8:31

Lots of things go on in the world that are not good.
The newspaper and the Bible tell of the world's evils.
The Bible also says God is FOR me! He is on my side!
No plans of the devil can defeat me!
I look to the Lord first in all I do.
I am strong in the power of His might!
If God is FOR me, WHO can be against me?!!

149   A good name is to be chosen rather than great riches.
Proverbs 22:1

God knew my name before I was ever born!
Jesus has my name written in His book in Heaven!
My family, friends and teachers all know me by name.
I will live in such a way that people
will think good thoughts when they hear my name!
They will remember me for the kind things I do.
When others think of me, they'll be happy to know me!

150   Rejoice in the Lord always. Again I will say, rejoice!
Philippians 4:4

I just love the Lord to pieces!
Words can't even tell how much Jesus means to me!
I praise Him all day long! I can't stop singing!
Jesus peps me up! He makes me feel good!
He likes me for who I am! His arms are always open!
He loves me, He wants me, He corrects me, He forgives me!
There is no one else like Jesus!

151

"And these signs will follow those who believe:
In My name they will cast out demons; they will speak
with new tongues . . . they will lay hands on the sick
and they will recover."

Mark 16:17,18

I'm a Believer!
Jesus gave a promise to all believers.
He said, when I speak in His Name
I have His authority.
If people want to be free of evil
I am able to help them.
If they want to be healed, I can pray
and God's power will heal them.
Jesus expects me to USE
the authority He has given me.
     I bring honor to HIS NAME
     when I speak HIS WORD
     and operate in HIS FAITH
to help those who have been beaten down by the devil.

152   For as many as are led by the Spirit of God, these are sons of God.
Romans 8:14

I am led by the Spirit of God.
He knows everything about me.
So He shows me what I need to know, step by step.
He gives me confidence in following His directions.
He fills me with knowledge of the Lord!

153   Likewise the Spirit also helps in our weaknesses.
For we do not know what we should pray for as we ought, but
the Spirit Himself makes intercession for us . . .
Romans 8:26

Lord, I'm constantly talking to You.
I'm ready to pray instantly when You need me to.
Thank You for the Holy Spirit inside me to help me pray.
I don't always know exactly how to pray, but You do!
You help me to pray just the right way
in Your language of intercession.
Thank You for helping me become a strong prayer soldier!

154

Therefore submit to God.
Resist the devil and he will flee from You.

James 4:7

In the Name of Jesus, I resist the devil! Get lost, devil!
I resist bad thoughts. I have good and happy thoughts!
I resist telling lies. I tell the whole truth always!
I resist rebellion. I am obedient to God and my parents!
I resist failure. I will work hard and be successful!
Jesus is the Lord of my life! I follow Him!

155

Let all bitterness, wrath, anger, clamor, and evil speaking
be put away from you . . . Be kind to one another, tenderhearted,
forgiving one another, just as God in Christ also forgave you

Ephesians 4:31,32

I don't let bitterness into my heart.
I do not remember wrong things that have happened to me.
Hurts and tears from the past are all gone.
I am tenderhearted and forgiving.
I treat others like God has treated me.
I walk in God's power, because I walk in His forgiveness.

156

But as we have been approved by God
to be entrusted with the gospel, even so we speak, not as
pleasing men, but God who tests our hearts.

I Thessalonians 2:4

God TRUSTS ME with His Gospel!
He has tested my heart and He knows I want to please Him.
I WILL please Him by telling His Good News everywhere!
I can't keep knowledge of God's love to myself!
I must, must, must share it with the world!

157

It is God who arms me with strength, and
makes my way perfect. He makes my feet like the
feet of deer, and sets me on my high places.

Psalm 18:32,33

The Lord is my strength!
I will trust in Him when I feel weak.
I'll receive His love, His guidance, His power.
No matter what kind of help I need,
I know my God will supply it.
He'll pick me up if I fall; then I'll keep going!
With God on my side, I cannot fail!

158

Give, and it will be given to you . . . With the
same measure that you use, it will be measured back to you.
Luke 6:38

I am a GIVER! I'm not selfish. No way!
I have a thankful heart, so I love to give!
I know God is happy when I give my blessings away,
because He keeps giving me more to give!
God and I both keep giving and giving!
I'm letting God use ME to spread His love around!

159

And if anyone does not obey our word in this epistle,
note that person and do not keep company with him.
II Thessalonians 3:14

I notice people who obey God.
I also notice those who don't obey Him.
I model my life after the wise people who serve God.
I don't keep company with those who are foolish.
I correct them in love. I pray for them.
But I only go around with people
who let Jesus rule their life.

160   Have mercy upon me, O God, according to Your lovingkindness;
according to the multitude of Your tender mercies,
blot out my transgressions.
Psalm 51:1

Lord, I know when I do wrong things.
Sometimes I try to hide them. But You always know!
The only way I can be happy again is to let
You know I'm really sorry for what I've done.
You always accept me! You always forgive me!
You clean me up and point me in the right direction!
I really try not to sin. But if ever I do,
I will always run TO You, and never away FROM You!

161   For whom the Lord loves He corrects,
just as a father the son in whom he delights.
Proverbs 3:12

Father God, I submit myself to You.
I want to do what is pleasing to You.
If I do something wrong, I want You to correct me.
You know what is best for me.
I will always give You power over my life,
because I trust You. Amen!

162

"As the Father loved me, I also have loved you;
abide in My love . . . that your joy may be full."
John 15:9-11

Jesus is my leader! I do what He tells me!
I walk in love toward everyone.
I show them how much God cares about them.
The more love I give away, the more joy I have!
Giving love always brings good results!
Love never fails!

163

I will both lie down in peace, and sleep;
for You alone, O Lord, make me dwell in safety.
Psalm 4:8

Thank You, Lord, for watching over me while I sleep.
I never feel alone! You are with me all the time.
My BIG, BIG angel is right in my room with me, too!
I'm not afraid of the dark. I'm not worried about dreams.
My dreams will be peaceful, bright, and happy!
Only good thoughts will come into my mind!
Good night, Lord!

164

> . . . from whom the whole body, joined and knit together
> by what every joint supplies, according to the effective
> working by which every part does its share . . .
> *Ephesians 4:16*

I am a part of the body of Christ.
The body of Christ means all of us Christians!
Jesus is the Head! He tells the Body what to do!
I have a special job to do to help the Body grow strong.
I'm the only one who can do my job in my special way.
God needs me. The body of Christ needs me!
I will do my share. Jesus can depend on me!

165

> . . . and every gifted artisan in whom the Lord has put
> wisdom and understanding, to know how to do all manner
> of work for the service of the sanctuary . . .
> *Exodus 36:1*

When God asks me to do something,
He will give me the ability to do it!
As I grow and try to please God, He will
show me HOW and WHEN and WHAT to do for Him.
I'm ABLE to succeed, because God's ability is in me!

166

*''If you can believe,
all things are possible to him who believes.''*
Mark 9:23

Jesus, I BELIEVE You died to give me eternal life.
I BELIEVE You were beaten so I could be healed.
I BELIEVE the power of Your Holy Spirit is in me.
Everything I need, I BELIEVE You will provide.
Power, Faith, Miracles—All are easy for You!
With God, nothing is impossible!

167

*Surely He has borne our griefs and carried
our sorrows . . . and by His stripes we are healed.*
Isaiah 53:4,5

I resist the spirit of infirmity in the Name of Jesus!
Devil, you can't put sickness on me! I'm God's property!
God doesn't give sickness; He gives healing.
Jesus was beaten with a whip for my sicknesses.
The Bible says BY HIS STRIPES I AM HEALED.
Thank You, Jesus, for what You did for me.
Thank You for a strong, healthy body!

168

Therefore we also, since we are surrounded
by so great a cloud of witnesses . . . let us run with
endurance the race that is set before us.

Hebrews 12:1

I have relatives who have already gone to Heaven.
They know whenever I do something that pleases God!
God lets them see whenever my life glorifies Him.
My great great grandparents are up there cheering
for me! They are praying for me, too!
They want me to be a winner for God!

169

. . . the Lord Jesus Christ who will transform our lowly body
that it may be conformed to His glorious body . . .

Philippians 3:21

When I get to Heaven I'll have a new body just like Jesus!
My new body will never get a runny nose!
No tummy aches! No measles or chickenpox! My new body
won't even get scratches if I fall out of a heavenly tree!
I will always be young, strong, and healthy!
I will never die! Hallelujah!

170

The eyes of all look expectantly to You, and You
give them their food in due season. You open Your hand and
satisfy the desire of every living thing.

Psalm 145:16

The Lord is full of mercy.
He hears the prayers of all who call on Him.
He has compassion upon the poor and the hungry.
He prepares food to send to their tables.
The Lord gives hope. His faithfulness is everlasting!

171

Do all things without murmuring and disputing.

Philippians 2:14

Complaining takes away joy. Yikes!
I don't want to lose my joy!
I'll try harder to be a cheerful helper!
I will clean my room and sing!
I'll do my homework with a merry heart!
I'm really blessed to be ABLE to do
all the things I am asked to do.
I'll walk in an "attitude of gratitude!"

172

(God has) raised us up together, and made us sit together in the heavenly places in Christ Jesus.

Ephesians 2:6

I'm flying high with Jesus!
God has raised me up into heavenly places!
Jesus is my pilot! He's training me to be His co-pilot!
He guides me through the dark clouds,
and shows me how to break through
into the brightness of victory!
Obstacles may be in my way,
every flight may not
be smooth . . . But
Jesus and I will
arrive right
on time!

173

Because Your lovingkindness is better than life, my lips shall praise You . . . I will lift up my hands in Your name.

Psalm 63:3,4

Dear Lord, You are my God!
I remember You early in the morning.
I think about You as I go to sleep at night.
Your love for me fills my heart with music!
My lips will sing praise to Your mighty Name!
I will lift up my hands and rejoice!
There is no one as wonderful as my God!

174

> In the multitude of words sin is not lacking,
> but he who restrains his lips is wise.
> *Proverbs 10:19*

I look for good things to talk about.
I don't tell bad reports about other people.
If I can't say something nice,
I just won't say anything at all.
I am a peacemaker! I'm a giver of good news!

175

> "Judge not, that you be not judged.
> For with what judgment you judge, you will be judged."
> *Matthew 7:1,2a*

I will not judge other people.
I don't know what is in someone else's heart.
My job is not to criticize others.
My job is to share God's love and forgiveness!
I'll be someone others can talk to.
Someone they can trust.
When their heart is ready, I'll be
able to lead them to the Lord.

176 "Everyone who exalts himself will be abased,
and he who humbles himself will be exalted."
Luke 18:14b

My righteousness comes from my Lord, Jesus Christ!
Any goodness I have is from His Spirit in me.
I need God's help every day!
God gives me the desire to do His will.
Jesus is the source of all my power!
Without Him I can do nothing . . .
But WITH HIM I can do anything He asks!

177 O Lord, You have searched me and known me . . . You understand
my thought afar off . . . You are acquainted with all my ways.
Psalm 139:1-3

Lord, You know me better than anyone else.
You search my heart. You know my inner thoughts.
You know when I'm awake or asleep.
You understand all of my concerns.
You are aware of all my hopes, needs, and desires.
You're always with me, loving me, thinking about me,
and caring for me.
Thank You, precious Lord. I love You.

178
And blessed is he who is not offended because of Me.
Luke 7:23

I am proud to be a Christian!
My life is a joy because I know Jesus!
How could I deny Jesus when He's my best Friend?
I'll ALWAYS look for ways to tell others about Him!
I want the whole world to know
the most important Person in my life!

179
He who made me in the womb,
Does he not see my ways, and count all my steps?
Job 31:4,15

The God of Creation made me. He gave me life inside my
mother. He sees all my ways. He counts all my steps.
If I step out of His path, He warns me.
If I were in the darkest forest, He would see me.
If I were lost in a crowd of strangers,
God would know, and He would take care of me.
I put my trust totally in God.
No matter what situation I am in,
I KNOW my Heavenly Father will rescue me!

180   Bless the Lord, O my soul, and forget not all His benefits.
Psalm 103:2

I will bless You, O Lord!
When I think of You, my spirit man leaps for joy!
I could never forget all You have done for me.
You rescued me from the devil! You forgave all my sins.
You heal me whenever I get sick. You keep me from harm.
You crown me with Your lovingkindness.
Thank You, Lord! I'll rejoice in You forever!

181

Romans 8:37-39 (Personalized)

In all things I am more than a conqueror
Through Jesus who loves me!
For I am convinced that neither death nor life,
Nor angels nor principalities nor powers,
Nor things present nor things to come,
Nor height nor depth,
Nor any other created thing,
Shall be able to separate me from the love of God
Which is in Christ Jesus my Lord!

Note to Parents: A portion of the curse within the old law declared that the sins of the fathers would be visited upon their children even to several generations *(Exodus 34:7).* Many Bible scholars agree that this does not mean God punishes children for the sins of their parents, but that if unprotected, the child may be open to demonic activities which controlled parents, grandparents or other ancestors. The protection God provides is, of course, the blood of Jesus.

The following confession is lengthy but powerful. If there is any question of controlling problems or sins in the child's ancestry, I recommend that this confession be spoken over and spoken by the child. And because we know Satan will often leave for a season and then try to return, periodic faith-filled declaration of these words can certainly do no harm.

182   Christ has redeemed us from the curse of the law,
having become a curse for us...that the blessing of Abraham
might come upon the Gentiles in Christ Jesus, that we might
receive the promise of the Spirit through faith.
Galatians 3:13a,14

Father, Your Word says when I accepted Jesus I was redeemed from the curse of the law. Part of the old law said that sins of the parents would come upon the children for many generations.

I don't know all my ancestors. I don't know if they did bad or good in their lives. I want to be sure I have no curse from the devil on my life, because of anything someone else in my family has done.

So, in the Name of Jesus of Nazareth,
I break any power of the devil over my life!
I break the power of any sin from any past generations.
I resist any curse the devil has tried to put on
our family!

I am free in Jesus!
I'm a new creation!
I am washed in the blood of the Lord Jesus Christ.
No evil can hinder my life.
I have authority over the devil.
He has no authority over me!
Jesus, You are my Lord!
You live in me, and I live in You!
I am redeemed!
Thank You, Jesus!

183   The Lord is my shepherd; I shall not want.
Psalm 23

The Lord is my Shepherd.
I am His little sheep.
He takes care of me.
He sees all I need, and He provides.
He encourages me when I feel upset.
He fills me with His peace.
He guides my steps,
so I don't get tricked by the evil one.
No matter what happens in the world around me
I have no fear. For my Lord is with me.
He comforts me with His presence.
He anoints my life with
the power of His Holy Spirit.
He pours blessings all over me!
The goodness of the Lord
will go with me all the days of my life.
Then I will live in the House of the Lord
Forever.

184

Behold, the eye of the Lord is on those
who fear Him, on those who hope in His mercy.
Psalm 33:18

The eyes of the Lord are on me, because I love Him!
He watches over me because I trust in His mercy.
He keeps me from harm. He provides all I need to live.
The Lord is my help and my shield.
My heart rejoices in trusting Him!
I will bless His Holy Name forever!

185

We know that whoever is born of God
does not sin; but he who has been born of God keeps
himself, and the wicked one does not touch him.
I John 5:18

The devil can't touch me!
Because of Jesus, I am born of God.
I am GOD'S PROPERTY!
No plans of the devil can overtake me,
God leads me! His Spirit warns me! Angels protect me!
Thank You, Jesus, for Your power in me!
I have everything I need to overcome the devil!

186

Let love be without hypocrisy.
Abhor what is evil. Cling to what is good.
Romans 12:9

I will never pretend to love someone just to get my way.
I won't be nice in order to receive something in return.
I give love and kindness without expecting anything back.
I do it just so I can be like Jesus.
Jesus is good and merciful because He really loves us.
I will model my actions after Jesus.

187

Do not be unequally yoked together with unbelievers.
"Come out from among them and be separate, says the Lord."
II Corinthians 6:14,17a

I am a witness to unbelievers. I love and pray for them.
But Jesus said for me to be separate from the world.
I won't let myself talk or act like unbelievers.
I must keep my life pure and clean to represent Jesus.
I will choose friends who love Jesus. I will grow up
and marry someone who is a joyful, strong Christian!
We'll have a God-centered life and family in Jesus' Name!

188

> . . . forgetting those things which are behind and reaching forward to those things which are ahead, I press toward the goal for the prize of the upward call of God in Christ Jesus.
>
> *Philippians 3:13,14*

Jesus, You are the Healer of all bad things. You come to those who need You. You make them new again. You give hope and direction for the future. Thank You for taking away hurt from any bad things that have ever happened to me. I will not remember the bad, only the good. I put my hand in Your hand, Lord. I will be full of Your hope and joy, as we go through life together. Amen.

189

> How precious also are your thoughts to me, O God!
>
> *Psalm 139:17*

How precious You are to me, dear Lord.
I think about You all the time.
I remember how You died for my sins.
I think of the pain You felt, and the blood You shed.
I imagine what it would have been like to sit on
Your lap, with You telling Your wonderful stories.
Everything You did was just to let people
know how much God really loves them.
Thank You, Jesus. I love You.

190   For to me, to live is Christ . . .
Philippians 1:21

Lord Jesus,
You are the reason I was born.
My Heavenly Father wanted me to be alive
so I could accept You and become His child!
He wanted to pour His love on me
and give me an important purpose in His Kingdom.
I have joy and hope and excitement about the future!

191   Then Paul answered, "... I am ready not only to be bound,
but also to die at Jerusalem for the name of the Lord Jesus."
Acts 21:13

Dear Lord, Your disciple Paul loved You so much, he was
willing even to die for Your Name. He wouldn't deny You.
He would not stop preaching. Help me, Jesus, to be true to
You. Even if people make fun of me for being a Christian, I
will still tell them You love them. I would rather have a
few friends who serve You than a hundred friends who serve
the devil! Help me to be a good example to others.
Thank You for boldness and courage to always live for You!

192

Children, obey your parents in all things,
for this is well pleasing to the Lord.
Colossians 3:20

When I obey my parents,
that's one way of obeying God!
I make God happy when I listen to my parents.
He is proud of me and blesses me.
Obeying my parents is one way I can say,
"I LOVE YOU!" to them and "I LOVE YOU!" to God!

193

For out of the abundance of the heart his mouth speaks.
Luke 6:45b

Whatever goes through my eyes or ears goes into my heart.
I have a watchguard on my heart! I read only nice books.
I watch only wholesome programs on TV or videos.
I listen to happy, healthy music.
God's Spirit helps me to know
which things are good for me and which are not.
I do not allow evil to get into my spirit.
My heart is full of good treasures!

194

Great peace have those who love
Your law, and nothing causes them to stumble.
Psalm 119:165

I rejoice in God's Word, as one who finds great treasure.
I love God's Word because God tells the truth!
I have great peace, because God's Word is in me.
Even if I make mistakes, God helps me out.
He never laughs at me. He's always there to lift me up.
Nothing can cause me to fail in life,
because I put God first!

195

Moreover the law entered that the offense might
abound. But where sin abounded, grace abounded much more.
Romans 5:20

Thank You, Lord that I have a free will.
I want to make the right choices, but sometimes I don't.
When I make wrong decisions, You are still with me.
Your Spirit hugs me and loves me and forgives me.
I always feel Your comfort and Your peace when
I say, "I'm sorry, Lord." You always make things OK again.

196

> He who has pity on the poor lends to the
> Lord, and He will pay back what he has given.
> *Proverbs 19:17*

I am so-o-o blessed!
I have more than I need of about everything!
I feel sad when I think of children who don't have enough
clothes to wear, or food to eat, or toys to play with.
I will share from all I have. I'll be a giver of blessings.
The Lord will bless me back, and then I'll give some more!

197

> For the wages of sin is death, but the gift
> of God is eternal life in Christ Jesus our Lord.
> *Romans 6:23*

Lord, in Jesus' Name I pray for those who don't know You.
Send Your workers everywhere to help people get born again.
Help me to be one of Your workers!
I don't want anyone to be lost.
Help me to show others Jesus is the way to eternal life.
Give me opportunities to witness, and boldness to speak!
Thank You, Jesus. I'll be working together with You!

198

But let patience have its perfect work, that you may be
perfect and complete, lacking nothing . . . Every good gift and
every perfect gift is from above, and comes down from the Father.

James 1:4,17

I am growing in patience!
I pray every day, for myself and for others.
Sometimes my prayers are answered right away,
and sometimes I have to wait.
If I have to wait, my faith stays strong.
I know God is working on everything I've asked
if it is based on His Word. By faith I receive
all the good and perfect gifts my Father has for me!

199

But you, beloved, building yourselves up
on your most holy faith, praying in the Holy Spirit . . .

Jude 20

My faith is holy to God.
God is pleased when I use my faith and trust Him.
ONE way I grow strong in faith is by hearing God's Word.
Putting His Word in my heart gives me spiritual muscles!
ANOTHER way I grow strong in faith is by praying.
The more I pray in the Holy Spirit, the stronger I get.
The stronger I get, the more God can use me!

200

> ''Assuredly, I say to you, inasmuch as you did it to
> one of the least of these My brethren, you did it to Me.''
> *Matthew 25:35,40*

When I give food to the hungry, I am feeding Jesus.
When I give clothes to the poor, I'm clothing Jesus.
When I give offerings so the lost can hear
God's Word, I am giving to Jesus.
Jesus loves every person so much, that whenever I bless
someone else, Jesus says I am blessing Him.
I AM SHOWING JESUS I LOVE HIM, BY
THE LOVE I SHOW TO OTHERS.

201

> Blessed be the Lord, because
> He has heard the voice of my supplications.
> *Psalm 28:6*

Lord, I bless Your Name!
You hear all my cries. You see all my tears.
You know all my needs, large and small.
My heart trusts in You, and You always help me.
Therefore, my heart greatly rejoices!
With my hands lifted up and with songs of joy
I will praise You!

202

"Take heed that you do not do your
charitable deeds before men, to be seen by them."
Matthew 6:1,5

Lord, when I do good things, it's NOT so people will see me.
I'll set a good example, so people can see YOU, not ME.
When I give my offerings, it's because I want to serve You.
The prayers I pray come from love in my heart.
I don't care about impressing people!
I want to do all I can to please You, because I love You.

203

"Do not be afraid; only believe."
Mark 5:36b

God has all power in heaven and earth!
He is always ready to use His power for me!
No matter what happens, I will trust God.
I believe in God's ability to work everything out.
All that concerns me is in His hands!

204

"Be angry, and do not sin:" do not let the
sun go down on your wrath, nor give place to the devil.
Ephesians 4:26,27

If someone makes me angry, I do not stay mad.
I forgive as quick as a wink! I don't stay upset!
Hurt and anger take away my joy, my peace, and my strength.
I won't let the devil get that kind of hold on me!
When I keep loving and forgiving, the devil scrams!
God's peace rushes in! I'm a QUICK FORGIVER!

205

"Whoever desires to become great
among you, let him be your servant.
Matthew 20:26

If I want to be great in God's kingdom, I'll first be a
servant. I will be loving even when others are unkind.
I'll be obedient when it would be easier to disobey.
I'll be dependable and not lazy. I'll use time wisely.
I am willing to give my time, my love, my life
to help God accomplish His will on the earth.
This is the way my life will have purpose and success.

206

Whoever has no rule over his own spirit
is like a city broken down, without walls.
Proverbs 25:28

My spirit is like a city with STRONG WALLS!
I guard what enters my spirit through my eyes and ears
so no evil can break down the walls of protection.
NO ENEMIES can come in to destroy God's work in me!
Good or evil can enter me through my five senses . . . so,
I'm making sure to let the good IN and keep the evil OUT!

207

Beloved, do not believe every spirit,
but test the spirits, whether they are of God . . .
I John 4:1

Jesus teaches me to test all I hear and see.
He helps me to know truth from lies. The devil is a liar.
Some people serve the devil, so they tell lies.
All things I SEE on TV or books are not always the truth.
All things that I HEAR may not be true.
I will listen to God's Word in my heart.
I'll depend on His Word to guide me.
God will keep me from being deceived.

208

Then we who are alive and remain shall be caught up
together with them in the clouds to meet the Lord in the air.
And thus we shall always be with the Lord.

I Thessalonians 4:17

I will always be with the Lord!
He is WITH ME while I live on earth.
And I'll be WITH HIM when I go to Heaven!
If Jesus returns to earth in my lifetime,
I'll go right up into the sky to meet Him!
He will take me and all Christians instantly to Heaven!

209

For if we believe that Jesus died and rose again,
even so God will bring with Him those who sleep in Jesus.

I Thessalonians 4:14

If Jesus waits a long time to return to earth,
and if I die like others who grew old and died,
I will just jump out of my body (like taking off a
coat!) and the angels will take me straight to Heaven.
The only people who can get to Heaven are Christians.
The angels will take them when they die,
or Jesus will take them when He returns.
Either way, I'm God's child, and there's
a home in Heaven especially for me!

210

For the word of God is living and powerful,
and sharper than any two edged sword . . .

Hebrews 4:12

The Word of God is powerful!
It is the mighty sword I use against the devil.
The Word of God is the answer to any problem I'll ever have!
All of God's wisdom is in His Word.
He put it into the Bible so it could get into ME.
God's Word will produce mighty results in my life!
I believe it, I speak it, I act upon it in Jesus' Name!

211

And now, little children, abide in Him, that when He appears
we may have confidence and not be ashamed before Him at His coming.

I John 2:28

Jesus is coming back soon! I'll be doing His will when He
comes. I'll be praying for the lost and telling them of
God's love. I'll be showing God's kindness. I'll be walking
in His Power and using the Name of Jesus to set people free
from the evil one. The Harvest is ready! I have a lot of
work to do! When Jesus comes, I'll be able to say,
''Yes, Lord, I did what You needed me to do!''

212

For the weapons of our warfare are not carnal
but mighty in God for pulling down strongholds . . .
II Corinthians 10:4,5

The earth is a battleground!
The devil keeps trying to win.
I am God's soldier!
I will do my part!
I have mighty weapons.
The power of the Holy Spirit is in me.
God's Armor covers me.
My mind is renewed by the Word of God.
I have power in my prayers.
I have authority over the devil
in the mighty Name of Jesus!
God is the WINNER
and I'm on God's side!

213

If then you were raised with Christ, seek those things which
are above, where Christ is, sitting at the right hand of God.
Set your mind on things above, not on things on the earth.
Colossians 3:1,2

Since my real home is in Heaven,
I set my desires on Heavenly things.
Nothing on earth is going with me to Heaven!
Heaven has plenty exciting things to keep me busy!
The only things I can take with me are human souls.
The best rewards I will have in Heaven are the people
who are there with me because I told them about Jesus!

214

And the peace of God, which surpasses all understanding,
will guard your hearts and minds through Christ Jesus.
Philippians 4:7

God's Peace is my peace! I have no cares!
God already knows about everything that matters to me.
My trust is already in Him. So everything will be fine!
Nothing that the world offers can give me real peace.
But Jesus gives me comfort way down deep inside.
Only the Lord can make me feel so good!

215

But he who is of a merry heart has a continual feast.
Proverbs 15:15b

I am a cheer-er-upper!
When Mother gets tired, I say, "I love you, Mom!"
If Dad gets cross, I understand. I give him the hug he
needs. I'm going to look for people I can cheer up!
No matter who I run into, my smile
can make someone's day brighter!

216

"The harvest truly is plentiful, but the
laborers are few. Therefore pray the Lord of the harvest
to send out laborers into His harvest."
Matthew 9:37,38

Lord Jesus,
I pray for You to send workers all over the world, to tell
lost people about God's love. Supply all the money
Your workers need. Give them safe travel.
Send them full of Your Power and Your favor.
Let every person on earth have a chance to know You!
Let me be one of Your helpers, Lord. Amen.

217

Fight the good fight of faith, lay hold on eternal life,
to which you were also called and have confessed the good
confession in the presence of many witnesses.

I Timothy 6:12

I fight the good fight of faith! I'm no quitter!
I keep on walking in love. I keep on praying.
I keep on sharing the Gospel.
Doubt isn't allowed in my heart!
The world won't take away God's plan for my life!
I will guard my words, my actions, and my integrity!
I won't lose, because God made me to win!

218

The Lord will perfect that which concerns me.

Psalm 138:8

Father God, in the Name of Jesus,
I declare that You shall direct my life!
I will hear Your voice.
I will listen to Your instructions.
I will know Your will in all matters that concern me.
Thank You, Father, that I am special to You.
You have a plan for my life that will be perfected!

219

Are they not all ministering spirits sent forth to
minister for those who will inherit salvation?

Hebrews 1:14

God has sent angels to earth to help us.
I can't see the angels, but they are everywhere!
They are BIG and they are MIGHTY!
When I have a need, I pray to God. If I pray in Jesus'
Name, and if I pray according to God's Word, the
angels get busy and help His WORD to be fulfilled!
Angels are just one of many ways God cares for me!

220

But we see Jesus, who was made a little lower than the
angels, for the suffering of death crowned with glory and honor . . .

Hebrews 2:9

God has angels working all over the earth.
One of their jobs is to protect me.
They can protect me when I'm being obedient to God.
But my trust is not in angels!
MY TRUST IS IN THE LORD!
Jesus has ALL POWER in Heaven and in earth!
Angels are mighty helpers for God, but
JESUS IS LORD OF ALL!

221

Many are the afflictions of the righteous,
But the Lord delivers him out of them all.
Psalm 34:19

God promised He would always be with me.
He said He would deliver me out of every trouble.
He didn't say my life would not have any problems!
He DID say He would help me overcome them!
I AM an overcomer! God is on my side!
Every day may not have blue skies . . .
But no flood is going to overtake me!
God and I can't sink!

222

For You are my hope, O Lord God; You are my trust
from my youth. By You I have been upheld from my birth.
Psalm 71:5,6a

In You, O Lord, I put my trust. You have watched over me
ever since I was born. Your love has never failed me!
I will grow up in the strength and knowledge of God.
My mouth will tell of Your righteousness.
When I am old and have gray hair, I will still
be proclaiming Your faithfulness and Power!

223

Is this not the fast I have chosen:
Isaiah 58:6

Fasting is giving up myself for someone else.
I can do without a meal to spend time in prayer.
I can give God's Word to those who are in darkness.
My money can help to feed the hungry.
When I give up SELF to help OTHERS,
the light of Jesus shines through me
and lights up the world around me!

224

Then you shall call, and the Lord will answer;
you shall cry, and He will say, "Here I am."
Isaiah 58:9

Fasting means I put God's desires first and not my own.
I look to see where I can be a blessing.
I treat every person as a valuable treasure.
I feel the love of God coming from HIS heart
and going out through MY heart to others.
This is why I'm so full of joy, and my
life has fulfillment and peace.

225
Therefore humble yourselves under the mighty
hand of God, that He may exalt you in due time, casting
all your care upon Him, for He cares for you.
I Peter 5:6, 7

I humble myself unto God. I realize I NEED Him.
I need His strength to lift up my faith.
I need His presence to give me comfort and hope.
I need His power to resist temptations from the devil.
I cast all my cares upon the Lord!
He can handle anything! My God has all the answers!

226
But I discipline my body and bring it into subjection . . .
I Corinthians 9:27

My body does not rule me! I rule my body!
I eat foods that are healthy and good for me.
I don't overeat! I don't fill up on junk foods!
I eat good snacks like fruit and juices.
I exercise daily. I make my body work hard!
I get plenty of rest so I can grow.
If I take good care of my body,
it will last me for a long, long time!

227

Do not lie to one another.
Colossians 3:9

I follow Jesus and not the devil! The devil invents lies.
He tells people in their minds that one little lie is OK.
But I have a choice! I choose not to listen to his lies!
Truthfulness is of God—and I belong to God—
so I tell the truth! People can believe what I say!

228

For we are to God the fragrance of Christ among those
who are being saved and among those who are perishing.
II Corinthians 2:15

My behavior is important to everyone around me.
Some people are just starting to learn about Jesus.
The things I do show others what Jesus is like.
The way I live my life may be the cause
of someone else changing their life!
I'll do my best to let them see Jesus in me!

229

(food) to be received with thanksgiving
by those who believe and know the truth.
I Timothy 4:3b

Thank You, Lord, for the good foods You give me to eat.
You provide all I need and even more than I need.
Help the poor, Lord Jesus. Use people who have plenty
to feed the hungry all over the world.
I will remember the hungry, Jesus.
I will be one who helps them.

230

Therefore by Him let us continually offer
the sacrifice of praise to God, that is, the fruit of
our lips, giving thanks to His name.
Hebrews 13:15

I praise God all the time!
Even when I don't feel like rejoicing,
I still praise the Lord because He loves me so much!
He has given me His life, health, joy, and victory!
He has already done all for me that I'll ever need!
PRAISE THE LORD!

231

But the wisdom that is from above is first pure, then
peaceable, gentle, willing to yield, full of mercy and good
fruits, without partiality and without hypocrisy.
James 3:17

I walk in God's wisdom. I keep my life pure and clean.
I walk in peace with others. I am gentle and kind.
I am willing to let others be first.
I don't criticize or talk ugly about anyone.
Because of God's wisdom working in me,
I am like a beautiful tree that produces good fruit!

232

But the Lord is faithful, who will
establish you and guard you from the evil one.
II Thessalonians 3:3

The Lord is faithful.
He causes His power to work for me.
He guards me from the evil one.
He directs my heart and guides my steps.
Because I want to obey and serve Him, God will
make my life happy and fruitful!

233

"If you love Me, keep My commandments. And I will
pray the Father, and He will give you another Helper . . .
(who) dwells with you and will be in you."
John 14:15-17

Jesus, I love You!
I SHOW You my love by keeping Your commandments.
I honor my parents. I respect my teachers.
I walk in love. I tell the truth.
I try hard to be like You in all I do.
Thank You for sending the Holy Spirit to help me.
With Him in me, I have Power to keep Your commandments!

234

And have no fellowship with the unfruitful works of
darkness...it is shameful even to speak of those things.
Ephesians 5:11,12

I don't talk about the evil that goes on in the world.
I talk about the good things that God does!
I say words that give people hope.
I show others the way to God's peace.
I let them know there is nothing too big for God to handle!

235

For whom the Lord loves He chastens.
Hebrews 12:6

If I do something that doesn't please God, I know it.
God tells me in my heart. I don't feel happy inside.
That's my CONSCIENCE. God corrects me
because He's my Heavenly Father and He loves me.
He wants me to be obedient so I'll have a happy life.
Whenever I'm wrong I go to God and repent.
He always forgives me. He fills me back up with joy!

236

For whatever is born of God overcomes the world. And this
is the victory that has overcome the world—our faith.
I John 5:4

I am an overcomer!
I overcome the world because I believe on Jesus!
My faith is based on God's Word. I BELIEVE for
victory even when I don't SEE the answer yet.
Faith rises up because I KNOW God can't fail!
He will solve every problem right on time!

237

Praise the Lord! For it is good to sing praises to our God;
for it is pleasant, and praise is beautiful.
Psalms 147:1

My Lord is great and mighty in power! He gathers His people like a mother hen does her chicks. He heals the brokenhearted. He binds up their wounds. He counts the number of the stars and calls them all by name. He knows all the birds in the sky and provides for the fish in the sea. My God understands all things. He lifts me up and fills me with confidence. His love reaches far beyond measure!

238

Strive together with me in your prayers to God for me.
Romans 15:30

Father, in the Name of Jesus I pray for my pastor.
He is doing Your work and the devil tries to stop him.
Fill Pastor with Your strength and vision and power!
Do Your will in our church, Lord.
Protect Pastor and all his family from harm.
Thank You for Pastor _____.
I love him and I appreciate him. Amen.

239

We are bound to thank God always for you, brethren,
as it is fitting, because your faith grows exceedingly.
II Thessalonians 1:3

I have exceedingly growing faith!
I think faith! I speak in faith! I live by faith!
Everything I believe is based on God's Word.
The more I HEAR God's Word, the more I GROW.
The more I USE my faith, the more God GIVES me!
Thank You, Lord, for increasing my faith!

240

Because he has set his love upon Me, therefore I will deliver
him; with long life I will satisfy him, and show him My salvation.
Psalm 91:14,16

Lord, I love You more than I can say.
I seek You first every day of my life.
If I have a problem, I call on You first, and You
always help me. You show me what to do and when to do it.
Because my eyes are on You, You make me a winner!
You give me protection and a long, healthy life!

241

Colossians 1:9-11 (Personalized)

Lord, based upon Your Word, I pray and believe
That I will be filled with knowledge of Your will,
That I will have wisdom and spiritual understanding,
That my life will be worthy of the Lord Jesus
And pleasing to You,
That I will be fruitful in every good work,
That I will increase in the knowledge of God,
And that I will be strengthened with all might
According to His glorious Power. Amen.

242

"But these are the ones sown on good ground,
those who hear the word, accept it, and bear fruit:
some thirtyfold, some sixty, and some a hundred.
Mark 4:20

My heart is like good ground. God's Words are seeds that
are planted in me. When I hear God's Word I keep it
in my heart. I let it grow, grow, grow in my life.
The seeds that God plants in me will produce a good crop!
My life will be full of good works that glorify His Name!

243

It is Christ who died, and furthermore
is also risen, who is even at the right hand of God,
who also makes intercession for us.
Romans 8:34

Lord Jesus,
It sure makes me feel good to know
that You are keeping an eye on me!
While You're on Your throne in Heaven,
You see whenever I need a little extra help.
You talk it over with the Father.
You send the power of God forth for me!
The angels listen to Your instructions.
I will always have whatever I need when I need it.
I walk in Your protection and Your provision.
My life is one of Victory!
Thank You for interceding for me, Jesus!
I appreciate You.

244
Yet who knows whether you have
come to the kingdom for such a time as this?
Esther 4:14b

I was born just when I was supposed to be!
God needs me right now at this time in history.
He has given me talents and abilities that
I can use in His kingdom in my own special way.
I am valuable to God because no one else is just like me!
I set my heart to be God's helper in every way I can!

245
. . . speaking to one another in psalms and hymns and spiritual
songs, singing and making melody in your heart to the Lord.
Ephesians 5:19

My heart is full of songs to the Lord!
I can make up psalms just like David of the Bible.
Melodies of praise come out
when I open my mouth in worship.
God made me to be an instrument of praise.
When I worship God, the devil gets scared and leaves!
I will praise the Lord my God forever!

246   "For in Him we live and move and have our being . . ."
Acts 17:28

Lord Jesus,
You are the most important Person in my life.
Everything that I am is all wrapped up in You.
You are interested in all that I am involved with.
You help me in every area of my life.
Living for You is what life is all about!

247   . . . even so in Christ all shall be made alive. The
body is sown in corruption, it is raised in incorruption.
It is sown a natural body, it is raised a spiritual body.
I Corinthians 15:22,42,44

I'm going to meet all kinds of people in Heaven!
I'll know them and they'll know me. My relatives and
ancestors, even people from Bible days will know me!
Everyone will have a new body like Jesus has.
We can run, jump and play, and ride a heavenly horse!
But our new bodies will never get tired or hurt!
And they'll never, never die!

248   "Therefore I say to you, whatever things you ask when you
pray, believe that you receive them, and you will have them."
Mark 11:24

Lord, You said in Your Word
for me to ask You for WHATEVER I NEED.
You're always interested and You want to bless me.
Whenever I ask, I ask according to what Your Word says.
I BELIEVE in my heart and SAY with my mouth
that my prayer is answered. Then, in Your perfect time,
You do it! Hallelujah!

249   Therefore, brethren, stand fast and hold the traditions
which you were taught, whether by word or our epistle.
II Thessalonians 2:15

I'm standing on God's Word!
My faith can't be shaken by what I see or don't see!
God pays attention when I speak His Word.
His promises were given in truth.
He ALWAYS fulfills His Word in perfect timing!
God's Words in my heart and in my mouth are mighty!

250

"I will . . . open for you the windows of heaven and pour out for you such blessing that there will not be room enough to receive it. And I will rebuke the devourer for your sakes."

Malachi 3:10b,11a

God is happy when I tithe! When I give part
of my money back to Him, He knows I appreciate Him.
I give to God by putting money in church to spread
the Gospel. What I give helps the poor and needy.
God opens the windows of heaven to pour blessings on me!
He keeps the devil from destroying what belongs to me!
I'm glad I'm a tither!

251

For it is God who works in you
both to will and to do for His good pleasure.

Philippians 2:13

Lord, I'm glad You know I'm not perfect!
You love me anyway!
You promised You'd HELP me to do Your will.
You even said You'd help me WANT to do Your will!
I really do want to please You, Father.
I'm glad we're working on me together!

252

I have set before you life and death,
blessing and cursing; therefore choose life . . . cling to Him,
for He is your life and the length of your days.
Deuteronomy 30:19,20

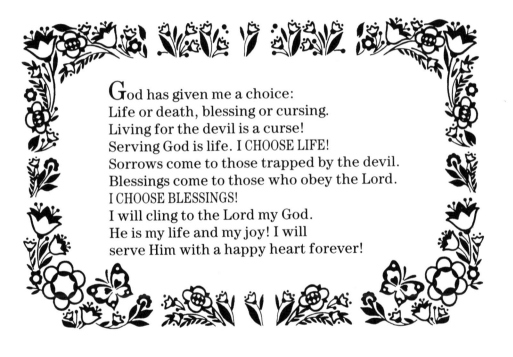

God has given me a choice:
Life or death, blessing or cursing.
Living for the devil is a curse!
Serving God is life. I CHOOSE LIFE!
Sorrows come to those trapped by the devil.
Blessings come to those who obey the Lord.
I CHOOSE BLESSINGS!
I will cling to the Lord my God.
He is my life and my joy! I will
serve Him with a happy heart forever!

253

Where can I go from Your Spirit? Or where can
I flee from Your presence? If I take the wings of the morning
and dwell in the uttermost parts of the sea, even there Your
hand shall lead me, and Your right hand shall hold me.

Psalm 139:7,9,10

My Lord and my God . . .
Where can I go that You are not with me?
Nowhere! Because You are ALWAYS with me!
If I could fly away to the farthest part of the earth,
Your presence would still surround me.
You hold me in the palm of Your hand,
Ever watching over me, tenderly caring for me.
I am Yours forever, Lord.
Nothing can ever separate me from Your love!

254

But you are a chosen generation, a royal
priesthood, a holy nation, His own special people . . .

I Peter 2:9

I'm a member of a special generation.
God is raising up a mighty army.
I am one of his soldiers!
I am one of many special people in His great army.
I will proclaim the goodness, the greatness,
the power and the praise of my God!
I will see God's glory fill the earth!

255

''Blessed is the servant whom his master will find
so doing when he comes. Truly, I say to you that he will
make him ruler over all that he has.''

Luke 12:43,44

Living for God is the smartest thing I will ever do!
The Creator of the universe is my personal Friend.
My life has a special purpose and plan.
God will help me with all He asks me to do.
All I have to do is obey!
If I am faithful, Jesus will give me
a position in His government when He returns.
I will be a ruler by the side of the King of Kings!

256

(God) comforts us in all our tribulation, that
we may be able to comfort those who are in any trouble.
II Corinthians 1:4a

If I see someone who looks sad, I'll go and cheer them up.
If someone is hurt, I'll help them. If they are confused
or upset, I'll tell them about God's peace.
I'll point them toward His Word. I will encourage
and comfort others the way God comforts me.

257

Grace to you and peace
from God our Father and the Lord Jesus Christ.
I Thessalonians 1:1b

God's grace is with me.
He leads me into blessings I haven't even asked for!
I don't do anything to earn God's grace...
He just loves me. He is so full of love
He is always pouring it all over me!
Thank You, Father! I love You, too.

258

And the prayer of faith will
save the sick, and the Lord will raise him up. And if
he has committed sins, he will be forgiven.

James 5:15

God doesn't want His people to be sick.
Jesus loved to heal the sick who had faith and asked Him.
God's Word says I can pray for the sick.
I pray in Jesus' Name and believe for God's power to work.
The faith God gives will cause the healing to come!

259

And my God shall supply all your need
according to His riches in glory by Christ Jesus.

Philippians 4:19

Because of Jesus I have no lack.
My family has no lack. We have all we need!
God gives good food, clothes, and money to pay the bills.
We share what God gives us and He keeps giving more!
We will always have what we need in this life!
And we will always be able to help others!

260

Oh, how great is Your goodness,
which You have laid up for those who fear You, which
You have prepared for those who trust in You.

Psalm 31:19

O Lord, my Lord,
You are my rock and my fortress. I have no fear!
You will lead me into peace and safety.
You keep me away from the devil's evil plans.
You are my strength. I trust You at all times.
How great is Your mercy, O Lord!
Your goodness will surround me forever!

261

''And from the days of John the Baptist
until now, the kingdom of heaven suffers violence,
and the violent take it by force.''

Matthew 11:12

Sometimes I just have to get MAD at the devil!
He may not want to listen to me the first time, so I
tell him again—LOUDER—to leave me alone!
I won't put up with the devil's ways!
Jesus has ALL POWER over the devil, and
Jesus is IN ME, so the devil has to SCRAM!

262   "Seek the Lord your God, and you will find Him if
you seek Him with all your heart and with all your soul."
Deuteronomy 4:29

I am not halfway in serving my God!
I honor God with my whole life!
All that is within me praises His name!
I will keep seeking and learning about Him.
I'll keep following the example that Jesus gave me.
My life will be abundantly blessed because God is first!

263   But if we walk in the light as He is
in the light, we have fellowship with one another.
I John 1:7

I walk in God's Light.
Jesus is the Light and His light is in me!
God surrounds me with friends who walk in His light.
The only true friends I'll ever have
are those who are serious about serving God.
I invite God into all my relationships with others.
Jesus is my first love, and I'll never leave Him out!

264

He who tills his land will have plenty of bread,
but he who follows frivolity will have poverty enough!

Proverbs 28:19

While I am a child, going to school is my job!
I am very serious about my schoolwork.
I pay attention. I complete my assignments.
I make up my mind to learn all I can.
School is fun and enjoyable because I'm doing my best!
I will earn rewards in later years by
putting forth my best efforts now!

265

''However, when He, the Spirit of truth,
has come, He will guide you into all truth . . . He
will show you things to come.''

John 16:13

The Holy Spirit leads me into paths of righteousness.
He keeps me from falling into traps of the devil.
He warns me when danger is near.
He alerts me to physical danger—or spiritual danger.
I will listen to the voice of God's Spirit.
He will always tell me the right thing to do.

266

I have not hidden Your righteousness within my heart;
I have declared Your faithfulness and Your salvation.
Psalm 40:10

I declare the faithfulness and salvation of the Lord!
I don't hide His goodness. I share Him with everyone!
God's love is a treasure that increases.
The more I give Him away, the more love He gives me to give!
Keeping Jesus a secret would not bless anyone.
I'll spread the news that God's love never fails!

267

Do you not know that you are the temple of
God and that the Spirit of God dwells in you?
I Corinthians 3:16

My body is God's temple on earth.
The blood of Jesus has made me holy.
God's own Spirit lives in me.
I take good care of my body, because it belongs to God.
I keep evil things from entering and harming my body.
I will use my body to bring glory and honor to God!

268

> But the fruit of the Spirit is love, joy,
> peace, longsuffering, kindness, goodness, faithfulness,
> gentleness, self-control. Against such there is no law.
> *Galatians 5:22,23*

I am led by the Spirit of God.
I am growing good fruit in my spirit and in my life.
I walk in love. I am full of joy. Peace rules my heart.
I am patient. I am kind. Goodness guides my thoughts.
I am gentle. I have control over my actions.
I live by faith in God. I have a Spirit-controlled life!

269

> Do not speak evil of one another,
> brethren...Who are you to judge another?
> *James 4:11,12*

I do not judge others, whether children or grownups.
I don't spread bad news! Gossip hurts people!
If someone has done something wrong, I pray for them.
I confess God's Word over their life.
I will speak only good, positive words
so God's Power can work in them!

270   The effective, fervent prayer of a righteous man avails much.
James 5:16b

Because I belong to Jesus, I am righteous.
Nothing stands between God and me,
So He hears all my prayers!
I have powerful prayers. They are based
on God's Word, so they are full of power!
My prayers can change circumstances.
Problems have to go! The devil has to flee!
Blessings have to come!
I keep praising God for His answers
and keep believing until His will is done!

Note: When I was a child in public school, my 6th grade teacher required us to memorize Psalm 27. I was 11. When I was 17, my dad went away. Psalm 27 had been in my spirit for 6 years. But when I really needed it, its message of strength and comfort rose up like a mighty force within me. It has remained one of my favorite psalms. Thank you, Miss Annie Lee Crawford.
Ginny Goode Kite

271

The Lord is my light and my salvation; whom shall I fear?
The Lord is the strength of my life; of whom shall I be afraid?
Psalm 27:1

The Lord is my light and my salvation.
I have no fear.
The Lord is the strength of my life.
Nothing can pull me down.
When the devil comes against me,
he has to run away in terror.
For my God is with me!
No matter what happens in the earth,
I will be full of courage,
for my trust is in God!

272

One thing have I desired of the Lord, that will I seek: that
I may dwell in the house of the Lord all the days of my life,
to behold the beauty of the Lord and to inquire in His temple.
Psalm 27:4

My desire is to live in God's presence.
I seek Him with my whole heart. I want to know Him!
I want to live in the fullness of His love!
He is my loving Father, my gentle Savior, my Friend.
In times of trouble He will hide me.
He will lift up my head in faith.
I will rejoice in His presence now and forever!

273

When You said, "Seek My face," my heart said to You,
"Your face, Lord, I will seek." (Should) my father and my
mother forsake me, then the Lord will take care of me.
Psalm 27:8,10

Lord I follow You and love You above all others.
You never leave me helpless or alone.
Should anything ever happen to my father or mother,
You will take care of me.
You will give me courage and strengthen my heart.
I will see Your goodness all the days of my life!

274

I will extol You, my God, O King; and
I will bless Your name forever and ever.
Psalms 145:1

I will praise You, my God and my King!
I will praise You Jesus, Lion of Judah!
Every day I will bless You! I will tell
of Your greatness and Your marvelous works!
I will declare the glory of Your kingdom to the world!
Yours is the Kingdom and the Power and the Glory forever!

275

"For I have given you an example,
that you should do as I have done to you."
John 13:15,17

Jesus is my example! He taught how to be truly happy!
Real happiness comes from giving up yourself for others.
I can do the things that Jesus did.
I have God's love in my heart! His Power is in me!
I can pray for the sick, lift up the brokenhearted,
and show the captives of Satan how to be free!
I know true happiness because I'm a doer of God's Word.

276   And where the Spirit of the Lord is, there is liberty.
II Corinthians 3:17

I am free from the pressures of the world!
Jesus has made me free, so I can choose how to live!
I CHOOSE peace and joy and love to rule my life!
I CHOOSE to live in God's light!
No chains of the world shall bind me!
I am free to enjoy the fullness of the Lord!

277   . . . bearing with one another, and forgiving one
another, if anyone has a complaint against another . . .
Colossians 3:13

I won't let people upset me!
Things others do will not make me complain.
I'll just forgive and keep smiling.
That's what Jesus does!
When I live in forgiveness,
God's peace can rule in my heart!
His peace overcomes all circumstances!

278

For where envy and self-seeking exist,
confusion and every evil thing will be there.
James 3:16

Strife is a work of the devil.
Being selfish leads to arguments.
Wanting my own way leads to anger.
I make up my mind not to let strife in my heart.
I resist the devil's work!
I am loving. I think of others more than myself.
I won't play the devil's game!
By walking in love I'm already the winner!

279

The Lord upholds all who fall,
and raises up all those who are bowed down.
Psalm 145:14

When someone sins, the Lord is right there
to take them by the hand, help them up, and forgive.
They only need to ask. No one needs to be afraid.
God is a gentle Father Who just wants to show His love.
So many people don't know God's tenderness.
I can help them to know.

280

Who Himself bore our sins in His own body
on the tree, that we, having died to sins, might live for
righteousness—by whose stripes you were healed.

I Peter 2:24 (Matthew 8:17)

Jesus bore my sins on the cross.
The Bible says He also took my pains and my sicknesses.
Adam's sin brought sickness, pain, sorrow and death.
Jesus restored life, health, and joy!
By Jesus' death I will live forever!
By His stripes I am healed! Instead of sorrow
I have joy unspeakable! Thank You, Jesus!

281

"Take heed, watch and pray; for you do not know when the time is."

Mark 13:33

Jesus is coming back to earth soon!
He's coming to take HIS people back to Heaven!
Lord, I pray for the people who don't know You yet.
Send ministers to take the Gospel to all people.
Use our nation to send Your Word into all the earth.
Keep me busy doing Your work, Lord.
I won't be loafing when You return!

282

Rejoicing in hope, patient in
tribulation, continuing steadfastly in prayer.
Romans 12:12

Father, sometimes the news on TV is scary.
Bad things seem to happen all the time, everywhere.
My hope is in You, Lord.
I put my trust totally in You and Your goodness.
I will pray, pray, pray for others and for myself.
Your peace will fill me and give me courage.
I am not afraid.
You have a plan for the earth, and You are in control!

283

Because you have made the lord your habitation, No evil shall
befall you, nor shall any plague come near your dwelling.
Psalm 91:9,10

Lord, You are always with me. I will never let You go!
I walk with You and talk with You. We are friends.
I believe Your Word that says "No evil shall befall me!"
No weapon formed against me shall prosper!
I am Your property! You keep me safe from harm!

284   . . . a man is valued by what others say of him.
Proverbs 27:21

People always watch each other.
They talk about what they see!
My life will cause good conversations!
I am not selfish or rude.
I am thoughtful and helpful.
My actions show others I care about them.
My goal is to let others see Jesus in me!

285   Be kindly affectionate to one another with
brotherly love, in honor giving preference to one another.
Romans 12:10

It doesn't matter who has the biggest cookie!
Having the front row seat is not important!
What matters is—do I think of others as much as myself?
Am I showing those around me
the kindness God wants me to?
When I treat others like Jesus would treat them
I feel really happy inside. God is happy, too.

286

And He said to them, "I saw Satan fall like
lightning from heaven. Behold, I give you the authority to
trample on serpents and scorpions, and over all the power of
the enemy, and nothing shall by any means hurt you."

Luke 10:18,19 (also Isaiah 14:12-14)

I know how to take care of the devil!
God already threw him out of Heaven!
And Jesus defeated him on earth!
Then Jesus gave me His Power and Authority!
The devil doesn't tell me what to do . . .
I tell him what to do!
I bind his work in the Name of Jesus!
I pray in the Holy Spirit!
I praise and worship Jesus with my whole heart!
The devil can't stay around me!

287

Choose for yourselves this day whom you will serve.
But as for me and my house, we will serve the Lord.
Joshua 24:15

My mind is made up! Jesus is the One I serve!
Every day I look for ways to please Him.
I choose friends who love the Lord.
When I'm ready to get married, God will
have someone for me who loves Him!
My household will have joy, goodness and peace
Because we serve the Lord of Lords!

288

''And blessed is he who is not offended because of Me.''
Matthew 11:6

I'm not ashamed of Jesus!
I'll stand up for Him even when others reject Him.
I'll pray for the ones who need to change their minds.
One day they will know the truth.
When they realize their life is a failure,
I'll lead them to the One who makes my life a joy!

289

Let not mercy and truth forsake you; bind them around
your neck, write them on the tablet of your heart, and so
find favor and high esteem in the sight of God and man.

Proverbs 3:3,4

I walk in mercy and truth. Mercy means I love all
people, no matter who they are or what they've done.
They will see that Jesus loves them, through me.
I am truthful. People can believe whatever I say.
Because I show God's mercy and truth, God is pleased,
And I find favor in the sight of God and man.

290

For You, Lord, are good, and ready to forgive,
and abundant in mercy to all those who call upon You.

Psalm 86:5

Whenever I'm in trouble, I run to my Heavenly Father!
He's always waiting to receive me with arms open wide!
My Father's love reaches me no matter where I am.
He is full of mercy and forgiveness.
His love never quits!
There is none as wonderful as my Lord!

291

Therefore I exhort first of all that supplications,
prayers, intercessions, and giving of thanks be made for all
men, for kings and all who are in authority.

I Timothy 2:1,2

Heavenly Father, in the Name of Jesus
Give President _____ Your wisdom and guidance.
Surround him with good counselors,
Men and women with godly advice to help him.
Protect our president and our nation.
Keep us in Your Light, so that we may surely be
One nation under God. Amen.

292

. . . I wish you were cold or hot.

Revelation 3:15

I'm a Christian and I want the world to know it!
I want everyone to know the risen Lord as I do!
I'm excited about serving the King of Kings!
My energy is dedicated to Jesus!
I won't grow cold or lazy. My fire won't go out!
Jesus is coming soon and I'll be ready!

293

A faithful man will abound with blessings.
Proverbs 28:20

I am someone people can depend on.
If Mom or Dad asks me to do a job, I do it.
I don't forget! I don't put it off until later!
I am faithful in my schoolwork.
I do my daily assignments without being reminded.
Because I am dependable, I am full of blessings!

294

One's life does not consist in the abundance
of the things he possesses. But seek the kingdom of God,
and all these things shall be added to you.
Luke 12:15,31

My life is more than food, clothes, toys, and vacations.
God gives me plenty good things because He loves me.
I don't need to worry about getting more and more.
I spend my time doing good in the world around me.
The things I have here on earth won't last long.
But the good I do in Jesus' Name will last forever!

295   There shall not be found among you anyone who
practices witchcraft, or a soothsayer, or one who interprets
omens, or a sorcerer, or one who conjures spells . . . for all
who do these things are an abomination to the Lord.
Deuteronomy 18:10-12

I will guard my soul. God's Word warns me that witchcraft,
magic, and fortune telling are tools of the devil. They
are DANGEROUS. These things deceive God's people
and get them into Satan's territory. I resist them!
I resist any influence of magic, witchcraft, or fortune
telling that has ever come upon any of my ancestors!
I am redeemed by the blood of Jesus Christ!
I am full of the power of the Holy Spirit!
Satan can't touch me, in Jesus' Name!

296   I can do all things through Christ who strengthens me.
Philippians 4:13

Jesus said He would help me to do anything!
I CAN be a good student with His help.
I CAN learn to read with good understanding.
I CAN think and reason and put thoughts together.
I CAN do number work with ease.
I CAN be good at whatever I set my mind to do!
All things are easy for Jesus, and He's my coach!

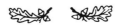

297

Therefore, as the elect of God, holy and beloved, put on
tender mercies, kindness, humbleness of mind, meekness,
longsuffering; But above all these things put on love . . .

Colossians 3:12,14

I am God's child.
I am loved and valued by my Heavenly Father.
Because I AM God's child, I ACT like God's child.
I have the nature of Jesus.
I am full of mercy and kindness.
I am gentle and patient in all my ways.
Above all, I walk in the love of Jesus for all people!

298

Let no one deceive you with empty words, for
because of these things the wrath of God comes upon the sons
of disobedience. Therefore do not be partakers with them.

Ephesians 5:6,7

I let the Word of God guide me.
I don't listen to suggestions from the devil!
I won't listen to bad ideas that may come from schoolmates.
Some kids do wrong things because they don't live for Jesus.
I know right from wrong! The Holy Spirit helps me
listen to God and do what is right.

299

Blessed is he who considers the poor;
the Lord will deliver him in time of trouble.

Psalm 41:1

Jesus has a special love for the poor.
He wants me to remember them, too, and help them.
God has blessed me so I can bless others!
When I share what I have, I spread God's love.
I make God happy and He pours more blessings on me!
He delivers me in time of trouble! He protects all
that concerns me, so I can show the world His goodness!

300

For even when we were with you, we commanded
you this: If anyone will not work, neither shall he eat.

II Thessalonians 3:10

I'm not afraid to work! Work can be a blessing!
Work helps me grow up into a useful, happy person.
Work doesn't have to be boring; it can be fun!
I will keep a cheerful attitude!
There are lots of things I can do to help at home.
I'll work hard in school, too! I will be
a valuable person: to myself, to others, and to God!

301

Do you not know that friendship
with the world is enmity with God?

James 4:4

My Friend, Jesus, is all goodness and light and love.
In Him are all the true treasures I will ever need.
The things of the world do not offer me much.
The world is full of sin and pain and sorrow.
I choose to be friends with Jesus and not the world!
I set my heart to follow the things of God.
He gives me real joy! He never lets me down!

302

"The thief does not come except to steal, and
to kill, and to destroy. I have come that they may have
life, and that they may have it more abundantly."

John 10:10

The devil is a thief! He tries to rob God's people!
Jesus is the Good Shepherd. He protects and blesses!
The devil lies. Jesus tells the Truth!
The devil gives sorrow. Jesus gives joy!
The devil makes people sick. Jesus heals!
The devil steals. Jesus provides all of our needs!
The devil is all bad. And Jesus is all good!
  I'M GLAD I BELONG TO JESUS!

303

He who keeps you will not slumber. The Lord is
your keeper. The Lord shall preserve you from all evil.
Psalm 121:3b, 5a, 7a

Heavenly Father,
You never go to sleep! You're always watching over me!
I can lie down and go to sleep in peace.
I have no worries or fears. Because I know
You won't let anything bad happen to me.
My confidence is in You!
Daytime and nighttime, I trust in You!

304

"This is the way you shall bless the children of Israel."
Numbers 6:23 (24-26 personalized)

The Lord is my God. I am His child.
The Lord will bless me and keep me;
The Lord will make His face shine upon me;
The Lord will be gracious unto me;
The Lord will lift up His countenance upon me,
And give me peace. Now and forevermore.

305

Deuteronomy 10:12-30 (Personalized)

My reason for living is to love and serve God.
I respect and honor my God.
I walk in His ways.
I love Him with all my heart and all my soul!
I keep His commandments.
For the Lord my God is the one great God.
He is mighty and awesome!
He is just and full of mercy!
I will hold fast to Him with all my strength!

306   And He said to them, ''Take heed what you hear . . .''
Mark 4:24

I pay attention to what God tells me!
I think about His Word day and night.
I will live the way He instructs me, so my life
will be prosperous and happy!
The more I USE God's Word, the more opportunities
He will give me to use it!
With His Word working through me,
I can change the world around me!

307   Do not grumble against one another, brethren . . .
James 5:9

I'm not a grumbler! Yuck!
Complaining is for the birds!
I am happy and cheerful!
People are glad when they see me coming,
because I share the joy that's in my heart!
I'm not a grouchy grump! I'm a pleasant praiser!
Hallelujah!

308

For He shall give His angels charge over you, to
keep you in all your ways. They shall bear you up in their
hands, lest you dash your foot against a stone.
Psalm 91:11,12

Thank You, Father, for Your angels guarding me!
I will confess Your Word, Lord, because the
angels listen for and act on Your Word.
I will be obedient, so I don't tie the angel's hands.
I will try hard to listen to You and to my parents.
I will be confident in You!
I receive Your protection day and night! Amen!

309

Honor your father and your mother, that your days may
be long upon the land which the Lord your God is giving you.
Exodus 20:12

When I obey my parents, I am obeying God.
I am always happiest when I obey!
When I'm listening to Mom and Dad,
I am walking in God's will. God can protect me!
He can keep me safe and give me long life.
Thank You, Lord, for Your Power helping
me to obey. I am blessed and I'm a blessing!

310

> "Therefore, whatever you want men to do to you,
> do also to them, for this is the Law and the Prophets."
> *Matthew 7:12*

I treat others like I want them to treat me.
I don't push or shove. I wait for my turn.
I'm not a tattletale. I am a peacemaker.
I am not greedy. I share.
I enjoy giving more than receiving!
By walking in Jesus' love, I'm truly happy.
Others know I really care about them,
and God can work in their hearts, too!

311

> There is one who scatters, yet increases
> more . . . The generous soul will be made rich, and he
> who waters will also be watered himself.
> *Proverbs 11:24,25*

I can never lose anything by giving!
If I give something away, the Lord gives me more!
I am sensitive to the needs of others.
I have joy in sharing with those who don't have enough.
I can give my prayers, my money, my toys or clothes.
I will never lack any good thing!
Because I remember others, God remembers me!

312
Let the word of Christ dwell in you richly in all wisdom,
teaching and admonishing one another in psalms and hymns and
spiritual songs, singing with grace in your hearts to the Lord.
Colossians 3:16

I am rich with God's Word! His Words are
treasures I will hold on to all my life!
Because of the Word of God in me, I am
a blessing to others! I encourage them!
I share the wonder of God's love and power.
I am happy that God can use me!
I will sing songs of praise to Him forever!

313
Trust in the Lord with all your heart, and
lean not on your own understanding; in all your ways
acknowledge Him, and He shall direct your paths.
Proverbs 3:5,6

I trust in the Lord with all my heart. Even when I
don't understand everything going on around me,
I know I can depend on God. He's my heavenly Father!
Jesus is my Friend! The Holy Spirit is my Helper!
The Lord will guide me all the days of my life.
I will grow up into His perfect will!

314

Now I urge you, brethren, note those who
cause divisions and offenses, contrary to the
doctrine which you learned, and avoid them.
Romans 16:17

Lord Jesus, I may have just
a few friends, but they'll be friends who love You!
I can love all people, but I can't follow their example.
Lead me to godly friends, Lord.
Thank You for putting good influences in my life.

315

Now, therefore, you are no longer strangers
and foreigners, but fellow citizens with the saints
and members of the household of God.
Ephesians 2:19

I'm a citizen of two countries! I am a citizen
of the United States of America (or other nation);
But eternally and forever I'm a citizen of Heaven!
I am a member of God's family.
All the other saints who have ever lived
are my brothers and sisters! We're ALL
citizens of Heaven! We'll have the biggest celebration
in the universe when we all get together with Jesus!

316

... and being fully convinced that what
He had promised He was also able to perform.

Romans 4:21

Because of Jesus, I'm just like Abraham!
God gave Abraham a promise that seemed impossible. But
Abraham believed God! He and Sarah received the promise!
I believe God gave promises so He could make them happen!
All the promises in the Bible are for people like me!
God will perform His Word when I believe and speak it.
The faith He gives me will bring it to pass in His timing!

317

For this cause everyone who is godly shall pray to
You in a time when You may be found; surely in a flood
of great waters they shall not come near him.

Psalm 32:6a

I pray to You alone, Lord. You always hear me.
When trouble seems to be all around,
it will not overtake me.
You are my hiding place. You keep me safe.
You surround me with Your presence. I am full of hope
and courage. Nothing can steal my joy!
The God of my salvation will never let me down!

318   It is impossible for God to lie. He who promised is faithful.

Hebrews 6:18, 10:23b

When God's Word says something, it's true! God can't lie!
When God says He will love me forever, I believe Him.
I KNOW I AM LOVED!
When God says He will provide for all my needs,
I say, "MY NEEDS ARE MET!"
When God says I am redeemed from sickness, I say,
"THANK YOU, JESUS, I AM HEALED!"
My faith is in God, because He is faithful!

319   Their sins and their lawless deeds I will remember no more.

Hebrews 8:12

There are two things God can't do: God can't lie!
I can depend on God's Word because it is true!
AND, God can't remember our sins
after we have repented and said, "I'm sorry."
God wants to DO only good FOR us!
And He wants to SEE only the good IN us!
So He gives us promises that He remembers! And
He forgets anything bad that would come between us!

320

Where there is no wood, the fire goes
out; and where there is no talebearer, strife ceases.

Proverbs 26:20

I am not a talebearer! I don't tattle or gossip!
If I see a person doing something dangerous,
I will let someone know to protect their safety.
But I'll use my words for good and not harm.
Telling bad news does no good to anyone.
I will bring good reports of good news!
I look for the good things in all people!

321

Brethren, if a man is overtaken in any trespass,
you who are spiritual restore such a one in a spirit of
gentleness, considering yourself lest you also be tempted.

Galatians 6:1

When I see someone sin, I'll remember that God loves them.
If it's someone I know, I will try to talk to them.
I'll tell them in a gentle way that God loves them
but He doesn't love their sin.
If they listen and repent, I'll rejoice!
If they don't listen, I will pray for them.

322

Do not associate with those given to
change; for their calamity will rise suddenly.
Proverbs 24:21,22

I will choose my friends wisely. Some people serve God
for a little while and then they serve the devil.
They keep changing their minds!
I have made up my mind! I'm going all the way with God!
I'll pick friends who feel the same way I do!

323

If it is possible, as much as depends
on you, live peaceably with all men.
Romans 12:18

I resist the spirit of anger in the Name of Jesus!
I refuse to let strife into my heart!
When strife comes in, joy and peace go out . . .
I won't let that happen! I'll forgive quickly,
even when the other person is wrong.
I'll be so full of peace and joy that
others can't even get angry around me!
Thank You, Jesus for victory over strife!

324

As each one has received a gift, minister it to one another
(and) let him do it as with the ability which God supplies.
I Peter 4:8-11

God supplies all my abilities. He gives me the ability to learn in school. He gives me special talents in music, art, sports, or other things. He gives me qualities from His Spirit like love and compassion. He puts His words into my mouth so I can minister hope to others. For all that God gives me I am thankful. Help me, dear Lord, to use my gifts and abilities to bring glory to Your Name!

325

But be doers of the word, and
not hearers only, deceiving yourselves.
James 1:22

I love to hear God's Word!
The Word of God refreshes me! It guides me.
It tells me what to do to be happy.
It tells me how to make others happy!
I'm not just a listener to God's Word . . .
I'm a DOER of the instructions He gives me!
I'm a tool that God can use to help change the world!

326

And we urge you, brethren, to recognize those who labor
among you, and are over you in the Lord and admonish you, and
to esteem them very highly in love for their work's sake.

I Thessalonians 5:12,13

Thank You, Jesus, for my pastor. Thank You
for teachers who watch over me and train me.
I love my pastor, Lord; and I pray for Your
Power and Grace to fill him.
I love my teachers. May Your will be
done through each one of them.
Thank You for my parents, too, Lord.
Protect them and fill them with
Your wisdom, Your joy, Your health,
and Your strength. In Jesus' Name.
Amen.

327

Instead you ought to say, "If the Lord wills,
we shall live and do this or that." But now you boast
in your arrogance. All such boasting is evil.

James 4:15,16

Lord, I place all my plans and desires in Your hands.
I ask Your advice concerning all I want to do.
I don't brag about things my family and I do, or
things we buy, or plans we have.
I am willing to say, "Your will be done" in all things.
May all that concerns us bring glory to Your Name.

328

And if you are Christ's, then you are
Abraham's seed, and heirs according to the promise.

Galatians 3:29

I belong to Jesus Christ, Son of the Living God!
I am redeemed from the rulership of sin. I am
redeemed from sickness. I am redeemed from being poor.
Because I belong to Jesus, my life is blessed!
No curse can come on me! I live an abundant life!
All my needs are met, for my spirit, soul, and body!

329

He who is faithful in what is least is faithful also in much;
and he who is unjust in what is least is unjust also in much.
Luke 16:10

I am faithful. I do the little jobs Mom and Dad
ask me to. I keep on working until I finish.
I do my best in school. I am dependable.
God is watching me! When He sees I am faithful in all
of these things, He will know He can trust me.
Then He will give me greater jobs to do for Him!

330

For God is not unjust to forget your work and labor
of love which you have shown toward His name, in that
you have ministered to the saints, and do minister.
Hebrews 6:10

God sees me all the time.
He smiles whenever I'm a blessing to someone.
If I give my money for the Gospel, God knows.
If I pray for God's people in need, He hears.
If I treat other people with kindness, He sees.
All the good things I do are pleasing to God.
I don't do good things to be noticed by people.
I do them to please my Heavenly Father!

331

For we do not wrestle against flesh and blood,
but against principalities, against powers, against the
rulers of the darkness of this age, against spiritual hosts
of wickedness in the heavenly places.

Ephesians 6:12

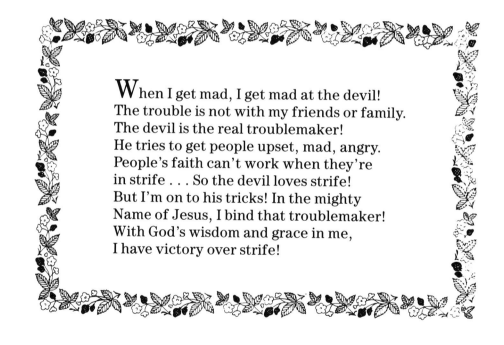

When I get mad, I get mad at the devil!
The trouble is not with my friends or family.
The devil is the real troublemaker!
He tries to get people upset, mad, angry.
People's faith can't work when they're
in strife . . . So the devil loves strife!
But I'm on to his tricks! In the mighty
Name of Jesus, I bind that troublemaker!
With God's wisdom and grace in me,
I have victory over strife!

332

But it is good to be zealous in a good thing
always, and not only when I am present with you.

Galatians 4:18

I'm excited about Jesus!
I love living for God!
My life is happy because I know who I am!
I know I have a special purpose.
God needs me!
I am super abundantly energized to
live every day all the way for Jesus!

333

Train up a child in the way he should go,
and when he is old he will not depart from it.

Proverbs 22:6

I am being trained by my parents.
I'm learning how to live a godly life.
I'm learning to walk in faith and love and victory.
I will never leave the Lord!
I will never depart from God's Word!
I will seek the Kingdom of God first,
Now and always!

334

And he who wins souls is wise.
Proverbs 11:30b

God says whoever wins souls is wise.
When I tell someone Jesus can help them,
I'm planting good seeds in their soul.
God can use every word I share in love.
He can cause those seeds to grow!
God has a special reward for soulwinners:

Those who are wise shall shine
Like the brightness of the firmament,
And those who turn many to righteousness
Like the stars forever and ever.
Daniel 12:3

335

Ephesians 3:14-19 (Personalized)

I bow my knees to the Father of our Lord Jesus Christ, from whom the whole family in heaven and earth is named, that He would grant me, *(child's name)*, to be strengthened with might through His Spirit in my inner man, that Christ may dwell in my heart through faith; that I, *(name)*, be rooted and grounded in love; that I may be able to comprehend with all the saints what is the width and length and depth and height and to know the love of Christ which passes knowledge, and that I may be filled with all the fullness of God. Amen.

336

A wise son makes a glad father.
Proverbs 10:1

Thank You, Lord for filling me with godly wisdom. With Your wisdom working in me, I will bring forth good fruit. My life will bring honor to Your name! The light You put in me shines on all those around me. My thinking, words, and actions make my parents happy!

337

If you extend your soul to the hungry and satisfy the afflicted soul, then your light shall dawn in the darkness, and your darkness shall be as the noonday, The Lord will guide you continually, and satisfy your soul in drought, and strengthen your bones; you shall be like a watered garden, and like a spring of water, whose waters do not fail.

Isaiah 58:10,11

I have compassion on the poor.
I pray for the needy and I give to help them.
I do my part to feed the hungry and homeless.
God is able to love others and meet
THEIR needs through ME.
Because I am willing, God meets my needs.
He guides my life into paths of joy.
He strengthens my body.
I am like a watered garden.
I will never dry up!
I will never have any lack
because my heart is extended to others.

338

Yes, I think it is right, as long as I am in this tent,
to stir you up by reminding you, knowing that shortly I must
put off my tent, just as our Lord Jesus Christ showed me.

II Peter 1:13,14

Peter was Jesus' disciple.
When Peter had finished his work for Jesus and was old,
he knew he would die soon. He was not afraid to die.
He said that dying was like stepping out of a tent.
The tent represented his earthly body.
When Peter died, the REAL Peter (his spirit man)
stepped out of his body just like walking out of a tent.
He went right to Heaven!
He didn't mind leaving the old tent (his body) behind,
because Jesus had a new body for Him.
When you belong to Jesus, you don't have to
be afraid to die! Because you go right from
this earth to your new home in Heaven!

339

For what is our hope, or joy, or crown of
rejoicing? Is it not even you in the presence
of our Lord Jesus Christ at His coming?

I Thessalonians 2:19

My HOPE is to live a life totally for Jesus.
My JOY is in knowing the King of the
universe as my personal Friend and Savior!
My JOB is to share Him with the world.
My CROWN will be seeing people in Heaven
who are there because
I showed them the love of Jesus!

340

Continue earnestly in prayer,
being vigilant in it with thanksgiving.

Colossians 4:2

I am faithful in prayer!
I pray daily for my family, for my pastor,
for our nation and for the world.
I intercede for others when God leads me to.
He needs someone who will be obedient and pray
when there's a need for supernatural action!
My prayers can help put God's power on the spot!

341

"Are not five sparrows sold for two copper coins?
And not one of them is forgotten before God. But the
very hairs of your head are all numbered. Do not fear
therefore; you are of more value than many sparrows."

Luke 12:6,7

God loves me so much that He
knows how many hairs are on my head!
He loved me before I was even born.
He will never put me aside!
He will never forget me!
His love is greater than the ocean,
wider than the sky!
There are no words that can
tell how much God really loves me!
I will always be able to trust in His
love, because He will never,
never leave me!

342

Praise the Lord! Sing to the Lord a new
song, and His praise in the congregation of saints.

Psalm 149:1

I will sing to the Lord a new song!
I'll make up songs of praise from my heart!
I'll sing to Him as I lie in bed!
I am joyful in the presence of my God!
For He loves me, and He is pleased with me!

343

That the sharing of your faith may become
effective by the acknowledgment of every good
thing which is in you in Christ Jesus.

Philemon 6

My faith is effective! Jesus lives in me!
His power and authority have been given to me!
I am full of His compassion. I'm led by His Spirit.
Every good thing has been given to me so I can
walk by faith and help others walk by faith!
My faith brings good results in my life.
As I share my faith, there will
be good results in many people's lives!

344   Now may the God of peace Himself sanctify you
completely; and may your whole spirit, soul, and body be
preserved blameless at the coming of our Lord Jesus Christ.

I Thessalonians 5:23,24

My spirit, soul and body belong to the Lord.
Jesus has given me Power to control my actions.
His Holy Spirit lives within me and helps me.
The devil is my enemy. But Jesus is my Friend!
Jesus has already defeated the enemy!
Jesus in me makes me happy, strong, and able
to live a victorious life!
I will guard my spirit, soul, and my body
so Jesus can keep working through me
to bring honor to my Heavenly Father!

345

For there are three who bear witness in heaven: the Father, the Word, and the Holy Spirit; and these three are one.

I John 5:7

Father, I am a 3-part person and You are, too!
You are God the Father, God the Son and God the
Holy Spirit. I love You, Father God. I am Your child.
I love You, Jesus. You are my big Brother.
I love You, Holy Spirit. You give me comfort and help.
Thank You, Lord, for giving yourself to me
in so many wonderful ways!

346

Whom having not seen you love. Though now you do not see Him, yet believing, you rejoice with joy inexpressible and full of glory.

I Peter 1:8

I haven't seen Jesus like His disciples did.
But I don't have to see Jesus to believe in Him!
His Spirit lives in me! I can feel His love and
His Presence all the time! He never leaves me!
I'm bubbling with joy because Jesus is real to me!

347

Repay no one evil for evil.
Romans 12:17

Father, sometimes kids have said things that hurt me.
There have been those that hit me or threw something.
I forgive them, Lord. Even if bad things like that
happen again, I will still forgive.
I won't say ugly things back. That doesn't help.
I won't get anyone into trouble. I'll just try
to act like Jesus. And Jesus will work it all out!

348

Let no one despise your youth, but be an
example to the believers in word, in conduct,
in love, in spirit, in faith, in purity.
I Timothy 4:12

I'm not too little for God to use me!
I'm young, but I'm mighty! I am serious about
living a life worthy of my Lord and Savior.
I am an example of God's love. I am obedient.
I show good conduct wherever I go.
Faith is working in me. I have a pure heart.
Even though I'm young, my life is
an encouragement to others!

349

> And we know that all things work together
> for good to those who love God, to those who are
> the called according to His purpose.
>
> *Romans 8:28*

God caused me to be born at the right time and place!
He put me in this world for a purpose!
He made sure I had the equipment I need!
The Bible teaches me! Jesus is in me! The Holy
Spirit gives me Power to do God's work.
I believe that all of the gifts God has
given me are working together for GOOD! I am
working together with God to change the world!

350

> You are of God, little children, and
> have overcome them, because He who is in you
> is greater than he who is in the world.
>
> *I John 4:4*

I am God's property! Jesus lives in me!
Jesus is greater than the devil, who is in the world.
Nothing the devil might try to
bring against me can be greater than Jesus!
So I am not going to be defeated! I am an overcomer!
Greater is He who is in me than he who is in the world!

351

Let your conduct be without covetousness,
and be content with such things as you have.

Hebrews 13:5a

Jesus is the most valuable possession I have.
He is my greatest treasure! My heart does not envy
people who are richer than I am. I don't worry about
kids who have more toys or bigger houses than I do.
I am content! I am thankful for every blessing
that God and my parents give me. I will always
remember: Jesus is the greatest gift of all—
because He gave me Himself!

352

By this we know love, because He laid down His life for us.
And we also ought to lay down our lives for the brethren.

I John 3:16,17

Jesus left His home in Heaven and came to earth for me.
He left the riches and glory and beauty there,
to walk the dusty roads of earth and tell of God's love.
He was the Creator of life, Who laid down His life for me.
Jesus really loves me.
I will give up my life too, for Jesus.
I'll give it up by living for others and not myself.
I'll give my time, my love, my prayers, my money.
God's Kingdom will be larger because I give.

353

For everyone to whom much is given, from
him much will be required; and to whom much has
been committed, of him they will ask the more.

Luke 12:48b

I am very blessed!
I have been given much.
I have God's Word in me as a child.
I have grownups who love me and are training me.
I have God's Holy Spirit and Power inside of me.
Because I have so many gifts, God expects a lot of me!
He needs me to be a faithful servant.
He needs my life—all I do and say—
to be an example of His love to the world.
I will walk in God's Faith and Love and Power!
I will use the gifts He has given me for His Kingdom!
I will be a blessing to this generation!

Note: These last scripture-confessions are written in such a way as to minister to the child's natural curiosity about Heaven, and also to impart the ''Revelation blessing'' which God promises to those who read and hear this powerful prophetic book.

354
Blessed is he who reads and those who hear
the words of this prophecy, and keep those things which
are written in it; for the time is near.
Revelation 1:3

I'm getting ready to be supernaturally blessed!
I'm learning God's prophecies in Revelations!
God tells all about His big plans for Heaven and
Earth! I'll be hearing His words and putting them
into my heart. My life will be full of grace and
peace, because I know what God's going to be doing!
One day soon, I will see Jesus reigning as
King of Kings and Lord of Lords. There will be
peace and beauty and joy in His Kingdom FOREVER!

355

> . . . and there was a rainbow around the throne,
> in appearance like an emerald. And from the throne
> proceeded lightnings, thunderings, and voices.
>
> *Revelation 4:3,5*

After Jesus takes all of us Christians up to Heaven
(see 208), I'll see GOD'S THRONE!
The beauty of His throne will be breathtaking!
Around it will be a rainbow. Lightning and thunder
and power will come from the throne. Thousands of
angels will be everywhere! Everyone will be shouting
praises and rejoicing to be in the presence of God!

356

> The city was pure gold, like clear glass. And the
> foundations of the wall of the city were adorned with all
> kinds of precious stones . . . And the twelve gates were twelve
> pearls . . . And the street of the city was pure gold.
>
> *Revelation 21:18b,19a,21*

I will see the Holy City of God!
My mansion will be there! God's city will be
more beautiful than anything I've seen on earth!
The city is made of pure, solid gold. It is
surrounded by a wall made of beautiful jewels!
The streets are solid gold, clear as glass!
The 12 gates are made of 12 GIANT pearls!
The only way through the gates is by knowing Jesus.

357

And the city had no need of the sun
or of the moon to shine in it, for the glory of God
illuminated it, and the Lamb is its light.

Revelation 21:23

Heaven is brighter than the sun!
The Glory of God and the Light of Jesus
are so bright there's no need for the sun!
There is no night in Heaven.
No one will get tired or need to go to sleep.
I'll never get bored! There are plenty of exciting
things to do to keep me busy!

358

And God will wipe away every tear from their eyes; there
shall be no more death, nor sorrow, nor crying; and there
shall be no more pain, for the former things have passed away.

Revelation 21:4

No one ever gets hurt in Heaven!
No one ever gets sick or dies!
Because NO EVIL can ever get into Heaven!
No one will ever cry or feel sad.
If anyone has been sad on earth,
God will wipe away all their tears.
He will fill everyone up with laughter!
We will be running and leaping with joy!

359

So also is the resurrection of the dead. The body
is sown in corruption, it is raised in incorruption . . .
We know that when He is revealed, we shall be like
Him, for we shall see Him as He is.

I Corinthians 15:42, I John 3:2

Everyone who goes to Heaven will get a new body!
We will still look like ourselves, but we'll have
a young, healthy, strong body like Jesus!
If anyone was crippled on earth, they will be
able to run and jump and play in Heaven!
If anyone has lost an arm or leg on earth, they
will have brand new arms and legs in Heaven!
Everyone will be totally whole and healthy forever!

*Thank You, Jesus, for leaving Heaven long enough
to come to earth and give all of us a chance to
become God's children. Thank You for all the
wondrous things You have prepared in Heaven for
those who love You! Happy Birthday, Jesus!*

360

Then I saw heaven opened, and behold, a white horse.
And He who sat on him was called Faithful and True . . .
Revelation 19:11

I will see Jesus sitting tall and majestic on His
beautiful white horse! I will see the glory of His
countenance and the gleaming crowns on His head!
He will be the one ruler of Heaven and Earth! He
will judge all nations. He will rule in righteousness.
There will be peace and brotherhood in the earth!
Everything in Heaven and earth will be the way
God wanted it to be from the beginning!

361

And the devil, who deceived them, was cast into the lake of
fire and brimstone where the beast and the false prophet are.
And they will be tormented day and night forever and ever.
Revelation 20:10

The devil's days are numbered! After Jesus returns,
He's going to finish Satan off! He will throw him and
all his followers into a lake of fire forever!
The devil will never bother anybody again!
Jesus will be King of Kings and Lord of Lords!
His Majesty and His Glory will fill all of Creation!

362

And I saw a new heaven and a new earth, for
the first heaven and the first earth had passed away.

Revelation 21:1

God is going to make a new earth.
After the devil is thrown into the lake of fire,
he will never be allowed in the earth again!
God will cleanse the earth from all evil.
Everyone and everything on earth will worship Jesus!
There will be no more wars! Everyone will be happy!
The earth will be full of the knowledge of the Lord!

363

And He showed me a pure river of water of life, clear as
crystal, proceeding from the throne of God and of the Lamb.

Revelation 22:1

I will see streets of gold and magnificent mansions in
Heaven! But there are also trees and flowers and grassy
meadows to play in. There is a river of crystal clear
water! It's called the River of Life! There is a
Tree of Life, too, with 12 kinds of fruit on it!
I'll be able to eat fruit from the Tree of Life and
go swimming in the River of Life! Yippee!

364

The wolf also shall dwell with the lamb, the leopard shall
lie down with the young goat, the calf and the young lion and
the fatling together; and a little child shall lead them.

Isaiah 11:6

All animals will be gentle and playful
in Heaven and in the new earth.
I'll have animal friends as well as people friends!
The wolf will eat grass beside the lamb.
The leopard will lie down beside the baby goat.
The calf and lion will play together.
The cow and the bear will be friends.
No one will ever get hurt in God's Holy Mountain!
Everything and everyone will be full of joy
and peace and love . . . FOREVER!

365

Revelation 19:11-14,16
Revelation 5:13

T hen I saw heaven opened, and behold, a white horse.
And He who sat on him was called Faithful and True,
and in righteousness He judges . . . His eyes were like
a flame of fire, and on His head were many crowns.
He had a name written that no one knew except Himself.
He was clothed with a robe dipped in blood, and His
name is called the Word of God. And the armies in
heaven, clothed in fine linen, white and clean,
followed Him on white horses. And He has on His
robe and on His thigh a name written:

KING OF KINGS
AND LORD OF LORDS.

And every creature which is in heaven and on the earth
and under the earth and such as are in the sea, and all
that are in them, I heard saying:

"BLESSING AND HONOR AND GLORY AND POWER
BE TO HIM WHO SITS ON THE THRONE,
AND TO THE LAMB FOREVER AND EVER!"

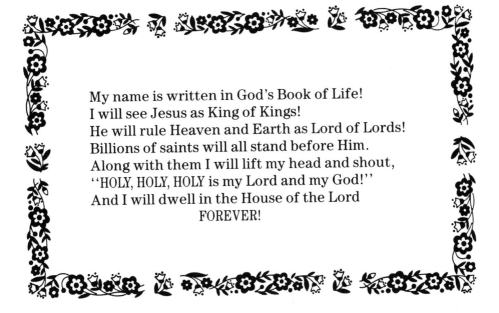

My name is written in God's Book of Life!
I will see Jesus as King of Kings!
He will rule Heaven and Earth as Lord of Lords!
Billions of saints will all stand before Him.
Along with them I will lift my head and shout,
"HOLY, HOLY, HOLY is my Lord and my God!"
And I will dwell in the House of the Lord
FOREVER!

But as for you, continue in the things which you have learned and been assured of, knowing from whom you have learned them, and that from childhood you have known the Holy Scriptures, which are able to make you wise for salvation through faith which is in Christ Jesus.

II Timothy 3:14,15

SUBJECT INDEX